Successful Machine Quilting

Marti Michell

Successful Machine Quilting

Marti Michell

Meredith® Press
New York

Dear Quilter,

Machine quilting has tremendous appeal these days as a beautiful, high-quality and time-saving technique. Now, in *Successful Machine Quilting*—a complete, step-by-step, illustrated machine-quilting manual—renowned quilting teacher and author Marti Michell explains (and demystifies) the entire machine-quilting process from start to finish.

With a winning combination of friendly prose, helpful illustrations, and the most authoritative, up-to-the-minute information available, Marti guides you through each technique-packed chapter, dispensing tips and insights that will build your confidence—as well as your creativity. Try out her methods on any of the sample projects that follow and watch how soon your newfound ability turns into stacks of beautiful, fun, and *finished* quilts and gifts.

Enjoy,

CAROL SPIER
Senior Editor

Special thanks are due to Pfaff American Sales Corp. for the loan of their top-of-the-line Pfaff Creative® 7550 sewing machine; thanks also to Horn of America for the generous loan of their sewing table, Model No. 1075 (and insert), information about which may be obtained by calling 800-882-8845.

Meredith® Press is an imprint of Meredith® Books
President, Book Group: Joseph J. Ward
Vice President, Editorial Director: Elizabeth P. Rice

For Meredith® Press
Executive Editor: Maryanne Bannon
Senior Editor: Carol Spier
Editor: Ron Harris
Associate Editor: Ruth Weadock
Copyeditors: Candie Frankel and Mary Butler
Production Manager: Bill Rose
Design: Ulrich Ruchti
Cover photography: Steven Mays
Cover photo stylist: Susan Piatt

For Quilter's Ink, Inc.
Illustrations: Ann Davis Nunemacher
Photography: Bread and Butter Studio, Atlanta
Photo styling: Stacy Michell and Marti Michell
Editorial Assistant: Jenny Lynn Price

ISBN: 0-696-02400-4 (hard cover); ISBN: 0-696-20432-0 (soft cover)
First Printing: 1995
Library of Congress Card Catalog Number: 93-077497

Printed in the United States of America
10 9 8 7 6 5 4 3 2 1

All of us at Meredith® Press are dedicated to offering you, our customer, the best books we can create. We are particularly concerned that all of the instructions for making projects are clear and accurate. Please address your correspondence to Customer Service, Meredith® Press, Meredith Corporation, 150 East 52nd Street, New York, NY 10022.

If you would like to order additional copies of any of our books, call 1-800-678-8091, or check with your local bookstore.

ACKNOWLEDGMENTS

It takes many people to complete a project of this size. For this book, my gratitude begins with all of those who contributed to the invention of the sewing machine, as well as those who have developed it into the wonderful tool it is today.

It is especially important to acknowledge and thank those who have been directly involved in the completion of this book. Several guest projects are featured, and those designers are duly recognized in the text. The rest of the projects were designed and made in my studio. For design assistance, special thanks to Ann Davis Nunemacher, particularly for the graceful feathered designs. The quilting and sewing assistance of the following Marti Michell Studio associates is also greatly appreciated: Ann Cookston, Martha Dudley, Sheri Gravel, Camellia Pesto, and Ellen Rosintoski.

The editorial assistance of Jenny Lynn Price in my studio made completing the text a more pleasant and feasible task. Candie Frankel and Mary Butler followed up with a superb job of copy editing. The graphic design by Ulrich Ruchti has greatly improved the appearance of the text and its ease of reading.

Words are great, but an instructional book only becomes complete with good illustration and photography. Ann Davis Nunemacher has once again provided accurate and attractive illustrations. Stacy Michell had both a good eye and good ideas as she assisted in photo styling. Steve Rucker of Bread and Butter Studio is our guru behind the camera. And a special thanks to Storehouse, Inc., and Don Guthrie, Senior Store Manager of the Storehouse on Dawson Blvd., Norcross, Georgia, for providing beautiful settings for nearly one-fourth of our projects.

Without the continued confidence, effort, and support of all the people at Meredith Press, especially Maryanne Bannon, Carol Spier, and Ron Harris, this book would not have happened. Thank you all.

Marti Michell

CONTENTS

INTRODUCTION

THIS BOOK REALLY IS ABOUT MACHINE QUILTING

Quilting, in its most elementary definition, is the process of holding layers of fabric and batting together, most often by sewing with a needle and thread. The word *quilting*, however, is commonly used to cover the whole universe of quilt construction—from patchwork to appliqué—and when used in a book title, it can understandably be construed to cover many techniques. This book really does focus on the process of holding layers of fabric and batting together using a sewing machine needle and thread. A few other machine techniques and tips are included, but the emphasis is on machine quilting.

One assumption I made while writing this book is that you know how to use a sewing machine and probably own one. If you own a machine but don't use it regularly, you will need to spend some time getting reacquainted with its operation before the projects in this book make much sense to you. If you know how to sew but don't currently have a machine, or if you are looking for a new machine, this book will help you identify the features that will be important to you as you begin machine quilting.

Please Read. Even though I believe the photographs to be beautiful and the illustrations extremely accurate and well done, I really do write books in a way that assumes you are going to read the words, not just look at the pictures. If the one burning question you have about machine quilting is, "How do you get a great big quilt through that little hole?" go directly to Chapter 10, "Whole-Quilt Machine Quilting." It wouldn't hurt to read through the Introduction, Chapter 2, and Chapter 3 for an overview of machine-quilting techniques and tools before you jump ahead, but that is up to you. When your curiosity is satisfied, you can come back and read the rest of the book and learn other fun ways to machine-quilt.

Please Do. To help you better understand the machine-quilting techniques I am presenting, I've included a quilt project for nearly every one of them. If you prefer, the techniques are easily adapted to garments or craft items. There is a Chinese proverb:

> I hear and I forget;
> I see and I remember;
> I do and I understand.

My intent is to tempt you to try the methods yourself in a relaxed and fun way so that you can truly experience the potential of machine quilting. I've begun with the easiest methods and projects and progressed to the most complex. For purposes of this book, "easy" means the most like normal machine sewing. I

I've darned and darned until my fingers are sore, I'll be darned if I darn any more

QUILTS

hope that after you try the "complex" projects, they won't seem so hard after all. Just as "beauty is in the eyes of the beholder," it could be said, "easy is in the mind of the performer."

WHY PEOPLE WANT TO MACHINE-QUILT

In the last decade, machine quilting truly has come into its own. No longer viewed simply as a substitute for hand quilting, machine quilting is ripe with possibilities that quilters are eager to try. As the exploration goes on, we are recognizing that machine quilting is a different skill from hand quilting—faster, but not necessarily easier. In fact, most people who have tried both methods appreciate that hand quilting is much more forgiving. Quilting a no-pucker quilt that lies flat, for example, is much easier by hand than by machine. So why is machine quilting enjoying such a rise in popularity? I think there are a number of reasons.

- *More quilts get finished.* The reason people first turned to machine quilting is, of course, speed. Once quilt makers started piecing and appliquéing by machine, they began turning out quilt tops in earnest. It became discouraging never to have time to get all those tops quilted. To help quilters keep up with their prolific patchwork, the commonsense approach of quilting by machine entered the picture. Reluctantly, quilt makers turned to in-the-ditch, highly functional, nearly invisible machine quilting as the most logical way to get their many quilts finished.
- *Everyday quilts last longer.* When it comes to crib quilts or college dorm quilts that will need repeated washing, machine quilting makes a lot of sense.
- *Quilted gifts are more realistic.* Most people find it difficult to give away a quilt they have spent weeks hand-quilting. If you have ever given someone a handmade quilt but still think of it as "my quilt," you know the feeling. People who have never quilted cannot always appreciate the number of hours you have spent stitching by hand, and they may not know how to care for the quilt in a way that would please you. Rather than agonize over the fate of their hand-quilted work, many quilters machine-quilt almost all of their gift quilts as a matter of course.
- *You can stitch any quilting pattern.* In the mid-1980s, quilters discovered a way to be more creative: They dropped the feed dogs on their sewing machines, and suddenly, free-motion traditional designs, like feather quilting, were added to the machine-quilting repertoire. Emotionally, the stitching was still a substitute for hand quilting, but it seduced quilters everywhere with its beauty. It was great fun to listen in at quilt shows as visitors argued whether certain quilts were or weren't machine-quilted—especially when you knew they were! Some machine quilting is so elaborate that it crosses the fine line between machine quilting and machine embroidery.

- *You can showcase fabulous threads.* Invisible thread helped start the move to machine quilting, but it has been followed by decorative threads that are meant to be highly visible. Together they have added a brand-new dimension to machine quilting.
- *You can use your sewing machine creatively.* One of the most important developments of the machine-quilting evolution (or is it a revolution?) is that quilters have discovered stitches and special effects unique to their sewing machines. Many quilters have learned to look at the sewing machine with new eyes, seeing it as a tool not merely of convenience but also of creativity. While this book covers all kinds of machine quilting, the emphasis is on the unique-to-machine techniques. To me the excitement of machine quilting is that these techniques are constantly being updated, with new ideas and looks appearing on the quilt scene all the time. Exercise your powers of observation at the next quilt show you attend to discover the wonderful effects people are achieving with their sewing machines.
- *You can have fun!* Some people truly love to use their sewing machines. Finding something new to do on the machine is the perfect excuse to keep sewing!
- *You don't need to apologize.* As machine quilting has become more prevalent and more attractive, attitudes toward it have changed. In the 1970s most quilt shows would not even accept machine-quilted entries, but by the late 1980s several machine-quilted quilts had won Best of Show and Viewer's Choice awards in prestigious shows. If judges can award top prizes to machine-

quilted quilts, then it's time noncompetitive quilt makers also take pride in their machine-quilted quilts.

• *Trailblazers led the way.* Finally, machine quilting has benefitted from its trailblazers—those who saw the potential of machine quilting, weren't afraid to buck the crowd, entered their machine-quilted quilts in competition, and taught others what they knew. Without them this book would not be possible, nor needed for that matter.

MY PERSONAL PROGRESSION TO MACHINE QUILTING

Let me emphasize that I love hand quilting. I love its look, and when I have the time, I enjoy the process. But I have also learned to love machine quilting, both for the time it saves and for the sewing pleasure it gives me. As much as I love making quilt tops, I love finishing them even more. A stack of machine-quilted quilts gives me more satisfaction than a pile of unquilted tops. The purpose of this book is not to compete with hand quilting but to encourage you to become acquainted with machine quilting and its many enjoyable aspects.

When I first started quilting in the early 1970s, the prevailing attitude was that a quilt wasn't a "real" quilt unless it was hand-quilted. I didn't question this premise, since I loved handwork and enjoyed hand quilting. Then my husband and I started a company that produced patchwork kits and other products for quilters. My daily schedule changed dramatically, and time for hand quilting became a thing of the past. I denied this reality for a couple of years until I began developing Quilt-As-You-Sew methods. This compromise was a good one for me because it combined the actual process of quilting with the machine piecing I enjoyed so much. The best part was that none of the telltale machine quilting showed on the top of the quilt. (I went to great lengths to make sure!)

Early in 1979, while in southern California on business, I stopped in Santa Monica to call on a new store account. The store was owned by Mary Ellen Hopkins. I immediately liked her approach to quilt making and felt it was compatible with our company's goals of promoting productivity without sacrificing design. Eventually, I asked her to teach five-day seminars around the country to other shopowners, and she agreed. There was, however, one technique she taught that I found hard to accept. Mary Ellen's machine quilting was visible on the top of the quilt! Since most of the stitching was "in the ditch" and accomplished the purpose of completing the quilts, I begrudgingly accepted her technique. Luckily, it was only a matter of months until we discovered "invisible thread" and I was emotionally rescued. Greatly relieved, I found it easy to accept visible machine quilting on the surface as long as it was "invisible."

The next giant step forward for me came when Harriet Hargrave attended one of our seminars. Harriet had been doing machine embroidery and was very comfortable using her machine for free-motion work. When she started quilting, it seemed natural to her to adapt her free-motion skills to quilting designs. The look of her quilts really excited me. In my mind, machine quilting was about to come of age. Soon Harriet was also traveling for us and teaching heirloom machine quilting. I believe this period was a turning point in quilting. Since then Harriet has written books on machine quilting and machine appliqué and has traveled the world introducing quilters everywhere to her techniques. No one person has done more than she has for machine quilting.

The final step in my conversion came about because of the beautiful machine threads that have become available. They are easy to use in the machine and exciting to look at on the surface of a quilt. Actually, it was seeing some of the fun effects my daughter Stacy was achieving with metallic and decorative threads that made me examine them more closely and take a more contemporary approach to machine quilting.

So here I am, writing a book on machine quilting, without any pretense of being the most skilled or creative machine quilter working today. My role instead is to be the best writer I can be and to present ideas you can adapt and use to enrich your own quilting. My hope is that my enthusiasm for machine quilting is obvious and contagious and that one day you will enjoy machine quilting as much as I do.

1

A LITTLE HISTORY OF SEWING MACHINES AND MACHINE QUILTING

1851–1965

Many different patents and manufacturing steps were involved in the evolution of the home sewing machine. Elias Howe is usually considered the inventor of the sewing machine. In 1846 he received a patent, which he successfully defended in court, but he never did make a commercially viable machine. In 1851 William Grover and William Baker were awarded a patent for their double-thread chain-stitch sewing machine. As early as 1859 a reference can be found lauding the ease and rapidity of quilting on a Grover & Baker sewing machine. The Smithsonian Institution quilt collection includes an all-white quilt that was elaborately quilted with a chain-stitch machine. While the exact history of the quilt is not known, its design and the use of the double-thread chain stitch suggest it is a very early example of machine quilting.

In the 1860s the Grover & Baker invention succumbed to competition from new lockstitch sewing machines. The lockstitch model, still in use today, used one-third the amount of thread and produced less bulky seams. It is generally agreed that ten essential components make up a practical working sewing machine. These include a needle with an eye near the point, a built-in fabric feed, and a shuttle that carries the thread below the fabric. Isaac Singer developed the first machine to incorporate all ten elements, although he actually invented only two of them.

The first sewing machine designed for home use was produced in 1856, with 2,564 machines coming from Singer's factories. Nearly every component for each machine was made by hand by skilled craftsmen. The cost of a machine was $125, or about one-fourth the average annual family income of $500. Even for those with the foresight to recognize the machine's potential for reducing daily drudgery and conserving time and energy, the cost was a major hurdle to be overcome.

Finding a way for customers to afford his product was the economic problem Cyrus McCormick faced when he started to sell reapers in the mid-1800s. His solution was to split the payment, collecting a down payment and freight in advance and the final payment plus 6% interest on December 1, after the first harvest. McCormick is credited by many with inventing installment buying, but there are those who argue that Singer perfected it. If not, he certainly added a new twist: Why not rent a sewing machine and apply the rental fee to the purchase price?

This wonderful photograph, circa 1915, shows a modern "quilting machine" attachment for the treadle sewing machine. The quilt was rolled scroll-like, and the entire scroll moved as the quilting was accomplished.

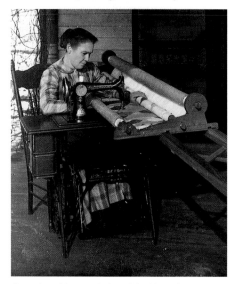

Reproduced by permission of the Kentucky Historical Society.

Sales under Singer's rental option increased favorably, and by 1858, three major sewing machine companies had produced approximately 16,500 machines. The very next year production was up to 41,500, and by 1862 an estimated 300,000 machines had been produced in the United States, 75,000 of them for private homes (the population was about 33 million). Despite the dramatic rise, it was only when mass production introduced lower prices that sales numbers really escalated. In 1870 the average price of a sewing machine had dropped to $64, and Singer alone produced 127,000. Even though the concept of domestic labor-saving devices was entirely new, sewing machines were making inroads, and the lucky women to acquire them were quick to show them off.

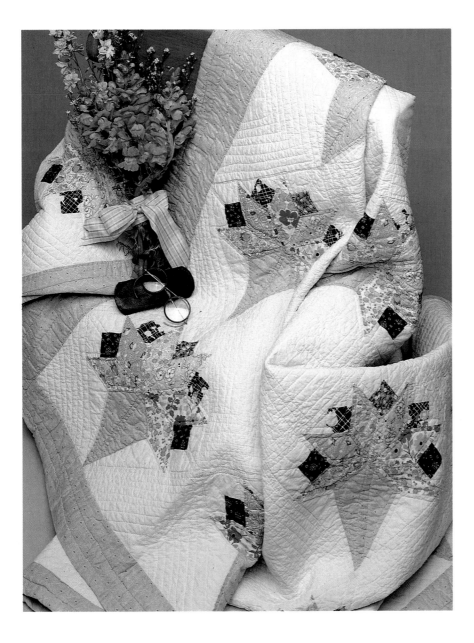

A Nosegay quilt, circa 1950, is the only machine-quilted example in our personal collection of vintage quilts.

While it is well known that home sewing machines were used to piece quilt tops, there is little evidence in the form of surviving quilts to prove that many quilts were ever machine-quilted. Why are so many antique quilts machine-pieced but not machine-quilted? My theory is that more women took advantage of machine quilting than is generally thought but that their quickly made utilitarian machine-quilted quilts were simply used up and discarded. The more beautiful or finely stitched quilts naturally would have been more treasured and given greater care over the years. These quilts had a better chance at survival, but they may be telling only part of the quilting story.

The main reason many antique quilts are machine-pieced but not machine-quilted may well be social. Social is one thing machine quilting isn't. If you have ever sat around a quilting frame and visited with friends as you hand-stitch, you know machine quilting cannot replace that pleasure. Quilters of the late nineteenth and early twentieth centuries were quick to accept machine piecing but not machine quilting, perhaps because it would have meant giving up the quilting bee tradition. I have no statistics to support this theory, but I do know that if I had been quilting in 1910, I would have used my machine to piece as fast as I could so that I would have had the excuse to have people over to quilt and socialize. After they left, I would have gone back to my machine to add the binding. But just like now, I would have probably done the final binding hem by hand.

1965 TO THE PRESENT

Quilt historians generally agree that World War II was the beginning of a serious decline in quilting. Perhaps the number of women joining the work force started the decline, but it was clearly fed by the availability of electric blankets after the war, a mania for modernizing that certainly didn't include quilts and manmade fibers. If you can remember polyester double-knits from the early 1960s through the mid-1970s, you know that cotton fabric for quilting was almost extinct. Most quilters of that era were not innovators but traditionalists who faithfully gathered at church quilting circles.

When the current revival began in the early 1970s, authenticity reigned, and rule 1 was, "A quilt isn't a quilt unless it is hand-quilted." In those early revival years as I gave public demonstrations on hand quilting, people would watch a while, then shake their heads and say, "Don't you think they could invent a machine that would do that?" Well, it is impossible to invent a machine that can *hand*-quilt, but machines have certainly been invented that can quilt!

One option, albeit an expensive one, is the commercial quilting machine. Most quilting magazines carry ads from several different manufacturers, and most larger quilt shows have at least one machine being demonstrated. With these machines the quilt is in a stable scroll format, and the sewing machine moves. As Mr. Gammill, the owner of one company says, "When you write, the pencil moves, not the paper. When you quilt, why not move the needle?" Some machines have dual controls, allowing the quilter to work from the side closest to the needle and to hand-guide the stitching completely or to work from the back using a template or pattern on the table surface as a guide. Quilting designs created from templates move across the quilt without regard for the pattern of the quilt.

This book deals with machine quilting on typical household sewing machines, not with commercial quilting machines. But even on household machines the capabilities have changed dramatically in the last ten years. Built-in decorative stitches, wider stitches, and computer memories are just a few of the recent changes that have opened up new possibilities for machine quilters.

A commercial quilting machine from the Gammill Quilting Machine Co.

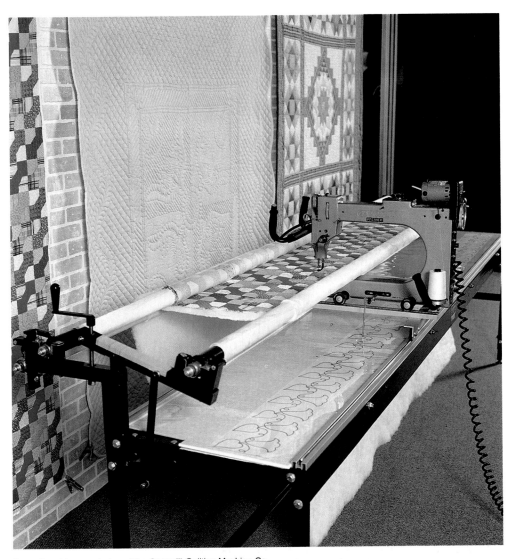

Reproduced by permission of the Gammill Quilting Machine Co.

2

AN OVERVIEW OF MACHINE-QUILTING CATEGORIES

FEED DOGS UP OR FEED DOGS DOWN?

When I started writing this book, I was naive enough to think that I could simplify the discussion of machine quilting by dividing everything into two categories: feed dogs up and feed dogs down. "Feed dogs up" means the sewing machine feeds the quilt under the moving needle. "Feed dogs down" means the quilt is moved solely by hand. While these two basic categories are not the whole story of machine quilting, they are a good place to start. Most machine quilters end up using several techniques in the same quilt.

What Are Feed Dogs?

Feed dogs are short rows of metal teeth that move up and down under the sewing machine's presser foot. In the up position they are responsible for moving the fabric through the machine at an even rate. In the down position they don't do anything. You may never have changed the position of your feed dogs. Don't be embarrassed if that is the case. In garment sewing, the most common reason for lowering the feed dogs is to sew a buttonhole. On newer machines the feed dogs often lower automatically when the buttonhole setting is selected.

To find out how to adjust the feed dogs on your machine, just consult your sewing machine manual. Some machines have a control that moves the feed dogs up or down; others have a metal or plastic plate that slides over the feed dogs to prevent them from making contact with the fabric. If you have lost the manual for your machine, check with the dealer to see if you can order a replacement copy. Make sure you have the exact model number, since many models look very much alike.

If your machine is old, you may find that there is no provision for dropping or covering the feed dogs. If that is the case, tape a section cut from an index card over the feed dogs so that they do not come in contact with the fabric. They will still be chugging away under the card, but to no avail.

In the Up Position

Quilt-As-You-Sew Quilt-As-You-Sew is a technique that allows you to piece and quilt at the same time. It involves layering the backing and batting together (often in block-size pieces) and stitching down the patchwork pieces on top of the layers. The completed blocks are joined with special finishing techniques to make a quilt. The beauty of the technique is that when you are finished piecing, you are finished quilting! You do not need a quilting frame, and most of the machine stitching is done on small pieces rather than on the fully assembled quilt. See Chapter 4 for Quilt-As-You-Sew projects, and Chapter 11 for ways to add Quilt-As-You-Sew borders. As you will discover, the method is not applicable to every patchwork design, but it can be adapted for most appliqué designs.

"In the Ditch" "In the ditch" refers to stitching in the space between two pieces of fabric that are sewn together. "What space?" you might ask. Granted, there isn't much, so you help things along by pulling the fabric on each side slightly away from the seam just before it passes under the moving needle. That slight tension on the fabric creates an extra-narrow channel for stitching. When your fingers release, the fabric relaxes and returns to its natural position and tends to hide the stitching "in the ditch."

On the Surface Sometimes you will use the "feed dogs up" position for stitching that shows on the surface. Examples include straight and lightly curving lines, grids, decorative machine stitches, and designs that do not include many turns.

In the Down Position

Free-Motion Quilting Straight-line quilting with the feed dogs up is really quite simple once you understand how to control the quilt and make it manageable. But what if you want to quilt in circles, as an extreme example? In traditional sewing, the feed dogs pull the fabric through the machine. Circles would require that you somehow rotate the whole quilt around and through the machine for every circle. No way!

Now is the time to lower or cover the feed dogs. With the feed dogs disengaged, the needle goes up and down but the fabric stands still—unless you move it yourself. You won't be able to move the fabric with the regular presser foot pressing down on top of it, so remove the foot and replace it with your machine's embroidery or darning foot. Lower the presser foot lever. You will see that the darning foot doesn't actually touch the fabric but stops a short distance above it. Now you can move the fabric around under the moving needle freely, in any direction you want, even in circles. The darning foot prevents the upward force of the needle from lifting the fabric, helps you see where the needle will be stitching, and serves as a safety buffer for your fingers. It is not absolutely necessary to use the darning foot, but I highly recommend it. If you decide to stitch without it, you must still lower the presser foot lever, since that is the same action that controls the upper thread tension. Although free-motion quilting may sound awkward, difficult, or scary, please try it. It is the favorite technique of most machine quilters.

MARKED AND UNMARKED DESIGNS

Like traditional hand quilting, designs for machine quilting are sometimes marked and sometimes not. Either approach can be combined with feed dogs up or feed dogs down.

Most marked designs are straightforward and easy to follow. The quilting pattern is marked directly on the fabric, and the quilting follows the marked line. Marking and sewing complex designs require additional skills and experience. Marked designs do take more time overall because the design has to be sized to fit the quilt, marked on the surface, and then removed once the stitching is completed.

Unmarked designs are basically created as you quilt. The stitching can correspond to seams in patchwork or appliqué, or it can take a completely free design. There are many easy ways to machine-quilt without marking, so we won't get to it for another few chapters.

MORE QUILTING CATEGORIES

In addition to feed dog position and whether or not a design is marked, other construction methods and design considerations can help you evaluate your machine-quilting options. Some may appeal to you more than others, but this book lets you try them all. Some methods and materials to be aware of are:

- *Quilting by the block.* Breaking a quilt into smaller sections, such as a standard quilt block, is not only a good way to ease into machine quilting but is sometimes the best choice for finishing a quilt that's been "in progress" too long. If you are trying to build the confidence to do an entire quilt by machine, a good place to start is to quilt by the block.
- *Continuous designs.* Continuous quilting designs are more appropriate to machine quilting than patterns that "stop and go." Hand quilters have the advantage of hiding the thread in the batting as they move from one line of quilting to another. Machine quilters must stop and knot, and then knot and start to make the same move. The procedure is time-consuming and leaves lots of thread ends to be trimmed. As a result, the emphasis is always on continuous-line designs in machine quilting.
- *Embroidery hoops.* Yes, even with the sewing machine, hoops can be used—not big quilting hoops, but small hoops used for machine embroidery, and generally for the same reason: to hold the fabric taut when the stitching design is very dense.
- *Invisible, matching, or very visible threads.* Improvements in "invisible" nylon monofilament thread and the proliferation of lovely decorative threads have contributed greatly to the popularity of machine quilting. The kind of thread you want to use can affect the technique that you choose. Or is it that the technique you choose determines the thread?

- *Decorative stitches.* Most newer sewing machines have an assortment of decorative stitches that can be used in machine quilting. The Fence Rail Sampler (pages 78–80) lets you try out the stitches on your machine.
- *Cotton or polyester batting.* Like threads, different fibers and weights of batting are suited to different quilting techniques. (For more on batting, see pages 33–35.)

Identifying a Darning Foot

I can't say I know anyone who has ever used a sewing machine darning foot for darning. In fact, an entire generation of quilters may not even know the definition of *darning*. Nevertheless, the people who design sewing machines believe that we are at home darning, so look under *darning* in most sewing machine manuals for information on how to prepare your machine for free-motion quilting. If you can't find an entry for *darning*, try *embroidery* or *machine embroidery* instead. Free-motion quilting will probably not be mentioned in either case, but the machine setting is the same.

The darning foot for your machine should resemble one of those pictured (Diagram 1). If you don't have a darning foot, a product called Big Foot™ can fill in for many but not all machines. Another option is the spring needle (Diagram 2). The spring holds down the fabric while the needle stitches. It is less expensive than a sewing machine foot and a good way to try free-motion quilting if you don't have a darning foot.

In case anyone who writes a sewing machine manual is reading this book, please look at the 1950s apron shown as an accessory in the photo on page 9. That early women's lib statement embroidered on an apron says it all.

Diagram 1

New Home

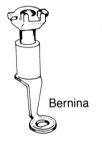

Bernina

Pfaff

Diagram 2

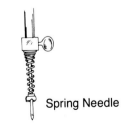

Spring Needle

3

TOOLS AND MATERIALS

THE MACHINE: WHAT KIND?

Nearly everyone wonders if they need a fancy machine to do machine quilting. Although I prefer my newer, top-of-the-line machine, I have successfully machine-quilted with all kinds of machines, from the very simple to the most expensive.

If you are thinking of buying a new machine, especially an expensive one, make sure you choose a dealer who offers classes on how to use it. The more expensive the machine, the greater its capabilities; therefore, the more its capabilities, the more you need classes to learn all the things the machine can do for you. Generally, classes are a service, not a profit center, and many dealers won't teach you how to use a machine unless you bought it from them. Don't fall into the trap of shopping around for the best price and getting stuck with a high-end machine with features you don't know how to use. You might shave a few hundred dollars off the purchase price, but if you are able to do little more than straight stitch and an occasional zigzag, what have you really gained? In addition to classes, a growing number of dealers sponsor clubs for owners of their machines. The club members meet periodically to share their own tips for using the machine. Of course, you should always buy from a dealer who can service your machine in case it needs a repair.

When you buy a new machine, don't trade in your old one unless you absolutely have to. Over the years I've kept every machine I've owned. It seems inevitable that no matter how wonderful my new machine is, there is always something about the old one—a stitch, a speed, a technique—that for some reason I can't duplicate. Besides, the old machine is available to take to classes or the summer place or to loan to a friend. When you are into marathon sewing, you will enjoy the luxury of having one machine with the zipper foot in place and another constantly set for a perfect hemstitch.

Buying a New Machine

If you are thinking of buying a new sewing machine, you may find the options confusing, the price range mind-boggling, and the compromises unsettling. Your decision depends on how you plan to use the machine and how much you want to spend. Here are some suggestions to help you narrow your search:

- Ask friends who have bought machines recently if they would purchase the same model today. Get their input about dealers, classes, and service.
- Spend time looking at several brands. Listen to the sales pitch but insist on getting answers to questions that matter to you.
- Make your own personal list of important features. The problem with a "wish list" is that it is often hard to know how much you want or love a feature until you use it! Once again, ask your friends, "What are the features on your sewing machine that you wouldn't give up?"

Quilters generally have their own special requirements for their sewing machine. A knee-lift presser foot, high-capacity bobbin, computer compatibility, large machine bed, and large neck opening are all features quilters typically seek out. If you truly need portability, decide on a maximum weight for your new machine. In this stage of my life, I do little garment sewing, and all my favorite features have to do with quilting. Here are a few (some have page references for further discussion):

1. Is the machine plate marked so I can sew an accurate ¼-inch seam without depending on a taped guideline? (This feature is more critical for machine piecing than for quilting.)
2. Is there a control that lets me stop with the needle in the up or down position, at will?
3. Is an even-feed feature or attachment readily available? Is it easy to put on and take off? (See page 26.)
4. Are the feed dogs easily disengaged for free-motion quilting? Is a darning or embroidery foot included, and is it easy to use and see through? (See page 21.)
5. Is there a way I can put this machine into a table or cabinet so that the bed is level with the tabletop? (See pages 27–28.)
6. Is the needle position variable? Are both straight-stitch and zigzag throat plates readily available? (See page 26.)
7. Is it easy to thread the machine and wind the bobbins? What about needle threaders? (I used to laugh at the thought of them, but with the combination of bifocals and decorative threads, I consider a needle threader to be a great feature!)
8. Is the satin stitch smooth, knot-free, clean-looking? When I was doing lots of machine appliqué, the infinitely variable satin stitch width was crucial.
9. What about decorative stitches? They never meant much to me until I started using decorative threads and got inspired by Iris Lee's machine crazy quilting. (See pages 176–179.)
10. Is the owner's manual easy to follow? Ask to see the owner's manual in the store and try to look up some of your questions yourself. Some manuals are much better than others, and when you get home alone with your machine, the manual will be very important.

THE MACHINE: GETTING TO KNOW YOURS

Perhaps more important than the machine itself is your personal relationship with the machine. You might say that machine quilting is a team sport. If you love your machine and already let it do hems and tucks and decorative stitching, machine quilting will probably be a snap. If you "hate your machine," trying to learn to quilt with it will probably send you to the funny farm. If you are always a little tense about your machine, unsure how it will behave on any given day, please spend some time getting to know your machine better before you start to machine-quilt, or find a new one you like better.

Start with a Cleaning

One of the easiest ways to get to know your machine better is to clean and oil it following the instructions in your manual. Even new machines claiming to require no oil usually need a drop in the bobbin area. Use your own best judgment about when to take your machine for a professional tune-up. Consider the age of the machine, how frequently it is used, when it was last looked at, and how it sounds, feels, and sews.

If you haven't put in a new needle for a long time, do it now, preferably a size 90/14 or 80/11. [No, the needle doesn't have to be broken to need replacing (see pages 29–30).] Select a spool of good-quality 100% cotton or cotton-wrapped polyester thread. Use the same spool to fill a bobbin and thread the machine.

Achieving Perfect Tension

Thread tension is more important in machine quilting than in traditional sewing because of the wide variety of threads that are used. Fine monofilament threads and decorative threads all have varying thicknesses, and it is sometimes necessary to make substantial adjustments in the tension when you change from one thread to the next. Every sewing machine has an upper tension control for the thread that goes through the needle. Most machines also let you adjust the bobbin tension. Getting proper tension in the sewing machine threads is a subject that can cause personal tension. Preventing that is our goal.

Why is tension important? The strength of your seams depends on it. When the tension is correct, the thread is perfectly locked between the layers of fabric, balanced so that it appears the same on both sides of the fabric (Diagram 1). If the upper tension is too loose or the bobbin tension is too tight, the thread on the underside will appear to lie flat on the surface of the fabric (Diagram 2),

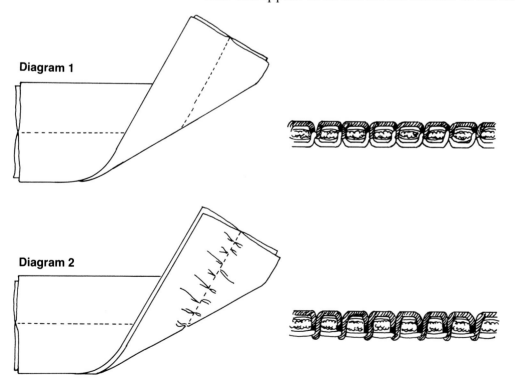

Diagram 1

Diagram 2

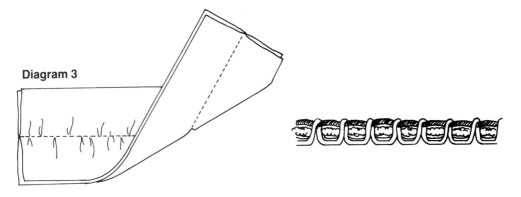

Diagram 3

and the seam will be weak and limp. If the upper tension is too tight or the lower tension is too loose, the thread will lie flat on the upper side of the stitching (Diagram 3), causing the fabric to pucker and the threads to break easily.

The upper thread tension is easily adjusted with a knob, lever, or dial marked with numbers or symbols. To loosen the tension, select a lower number, and to tighten it, select a higher number. Always adjust this control with the machine threaded and the presser foot down.

The bobbin tension control, if your machine has one, is a tiny screw located on the tension spring of the bobbin case (Diagram 4). Many of us were brought up with the idea that you never touch the bobbin tension (probably an idea developed by the same people who thought women shouldn't vote). Very small adjustments with a mini-screwdriver are usually all that's necessary. Adjust the tension after the bobbin case has been threaded, turning the screw clockwise to tighten the tension and counterclockwise to loosen it.

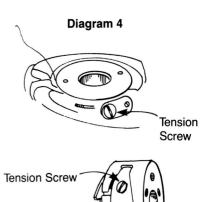

Diagram 4

Tension Screw

Tension Screw

If your machine has a removable bobbin case, you can easily determine whether the bobbin tension is correct. After inserting a thread-filled bobbin into the case and feeding the thread through the notched guides, pull the end of the thread to extend several inches beyond the case. Now hold the end of the thread and let the bobbin case drop (Diagram 5). A slowly descending bobbin case indicates correct tension. If the bobbin case drops quickly, the tension is too loose; if the bobbin case does not drop at all, the tension is too tight. Sometimes it is necessary to give the thread you are holding a little jerk to create the descending bobbin.

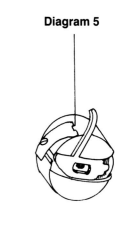

Diagram 5

Testing the Stitch Tension Every time you begin a project with a new combination of batting, fabric, and threads, you should test your stitch on scraps that are layered the same way. Tension is one of the first things to check if the quilt looks puckered or drawn up. When piecing, set the machine for 10 to 12 stitches per inch. For quilting, try 8 to 10 stitches per inch.

If your stitch tension sample does not appear correct, but you're not sure whether the upper or bobbin thread needs adjustment, try this simple test. Load the machine with different colors for upper and bobbin threads. Fold a square of fabric in half diagonally and stitch along the bias, parallel to the folded edge (Diagram 6). Hold the fabric at both ends of the stitching line and pull with an even, gradual force until the thread breaks. The broken thread is the one with tight tension. If both threads break evenly after more force, the tension is balanced. Once you have determined where

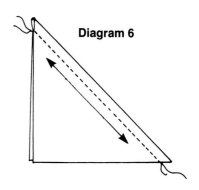

Diagram 6

the tension problem lies, rethread the machine and bobbin case with your project thread and fine-tune the upper or lower tension as appropriate until the stitch tension appears correct.

Do You Always Want Perfect Tension? Now that you understand and know how to achieve perfect tension, let me say that perfect tension isn't always desirable. More and more really creative quilters are allowing their machines to do a lot of the work for them. Some of the new techniques being developed take advantage of very distorted tension.

When I first started using invisible thread for machine quilting, the instructions were very simple. Put the nylon invisible thread on the top and cotton or cotton-wrapped polyester thread that matched the backing in the bobbin. It was almost always necessary with this combination to loosen the upper tension in order to have balanced stitches. Before I learned this, the too tight upper nylon thread would pull the bobbin thread up to the top of the quilt and make tiny puckers that mimicked tiny hand stitches. I used to joke that the best-looking stitch was created with bad tension. Then I would proceed to "correct" the tension and eliminate the tiny visible "hand" stitch. Recently, I heard that instructors were teaching this as a new technique. It does look convincing; but my conservative inner voice says that surely the stitch is very weak, acceptable for decorative pieces but not for those that will be washed a lot.

Diagram 7

High Shank

Slant Shank

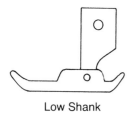

Low Shank

Even-Feed Attachments

When you have the feed dogs up and are working with multiple layers of material, the presser foot can force the top layers back as you sew. Nearly every machine has an even-feed attachment that helps move all the layers through the machine at the same rate. Basically, the attachment mirrors the work of the feed dogs on the top side of the fabric. Some Pfaff machines have a built-in even-feed, which I admit is my favorite feature for machine quilting "in the ditch" or anytime I have the feed dogs up.

To order an even-feed attachment for your machine, you will need to know whether your machine has a high, low, or slanted shank. Be sure you can tell the dealer the make and model number of your machine—or bring your machine in for a fitting. A high shank is approximately 1¼ inches high, a low shank is ¾ inch, and a slanted shank is used with slanted needles (Diagram 7). There are other variations as well, so once again, look for that machine manual. The more information you can provide about your machine, the better.

Straight-Stitch Throat Plate

Most sewing machines purchased in recent years have zigzag capabilities that require an extra-wide needle hole in the throat plate. The larger zigzag hole sometimes allows the pressure of the needle to force fabric into the hole. There may be times that switching to the straight stitch throat plate with its small hole will be advantageous. If you don't know how to switch the plates, check your machine manual and learn to make this adjustment.

A TABLE FOR THE MACHINE

When I write and teach, I like to offer many different alternatives, provide guidance and encouragement, and then step back and give people room to make the decision that is right for them, not me. I really don't believe there are many things that can be done only one right way. The proper table for machine quilting is one of the few things on which I thought I would always stand firm. The sewing machine should fit into a hole in a table so that the surface of the table and the bed of the machine are at the same level. No ifs, ands, or buts.

Then one day, in conversation with Debra Wagner (machine quilter extraordinaire), I learned that she lifts the machine out of the table and sets it at an angle, into a hugging position. When she first showed me this position, it looked so great that I rushed home to try it. I never got the hang of it, and because I already liked the way I was quilting, there was little incentive for mastering this new approach. Later I spoke with Hari Walner and discovered that she prefers a machine hole (like me) as long as she can quilt standing up. (Her hole is in a tall table!)

I've since concluded that the best approach is to try what is readily available to you now but to be open to other ways as well. Do remember that the position in which you sit and sew is crucial to your happiness in machine quilting. If what you try first is not comfortable, please don't give up machine quilting without trying some different solutions. Ideas to consider range from commercial sewing machine tables to improvised work spaces. Setting everything on a computer table puts the surface of the machine at a more comfortable level than regular table height. Fairly new on the market are adjustable-height platforms that sit on a tabletop around the sewing machine. They can be fitted with plastic inserts designed to fit the desired brand of machine.

A tabletop platform from Douglas Products extends the work surface of the sewing machine bed.

Diagram 8

Diagram 9

One of my favorite sewing tables was in a home with a large sewing room. The lucky owner had bought an old, fairly large, very sturdy kitchen table. She traced her sewing machine base on paper, transferred the pattern to the tabletop, and cut out the shape. Angle irons underneath the tabletop held a platform at just the right height for the machine. A variation on this idea is to make a special sewing machine leaf to drop into an expanding table (Diagram 8). When the leaf is added, it temporarily converts the entire table into a huge work surface for machine quilting.

It is wonderful to have a separate sewing room or area, but I always recommend that even if your space is limited to the kitchen table, you call it the studio. Somehow, working in the studio sounds impressive and elevates your efforts.

Using Extra Tables

If you have the space and the tables, you'll find it helpful to extend your table space when working on full-sized bed quilts (Diagram 9). Just butt the extra tables up against your sewing machine table. The extra work surface helps support the weight of the quilt. Without the support, you have to work harder to prevent the weight of the quilt from tugging on the needle and bending or breaking it.

Under the Table

Most sewing machines made today have foot-operated speed-control pedals that, unfortunately, scoot around. The scooting foot pedal is one of those things that you tend to follow subconsciously, contorting your body and stretching leg and back muscles in unnecessary and unhealthy ways. Most sewing machine stores and mail-order sewing catalogs sell a little rubber mat to keep the foot pedal stationary. Treat yourself to one and save your back.

Your Chair

Ideally, you will have a good five-legged rolling secretarial chair with an adjustable height and back support. Machine quilting puts extra stress on your back and shoulder muscles, so a good chair is very important. I like the adjustable-height feature, since it lets me look down on my work. In fact, when I really want a good sight line, I change to a medium-height stool so that I sit just below table height. I am actually propped rather than seated.

Protect Your Back

A good chair at the proper height, good posture, and a relaxed attitude about machine quilting go a long way toward protecting your back, shoulders, neck, and arms. Listen to your body, and if you get any signals of stress, respond. Frequent breaks will help you relieve muscle stress. When you are concentrating on stitching, it is easy to lose track of your position or how long you have been in it. Take advantage of the need to "repackage" the quilt (see Stitching Order, page 188) to stretch and gently rotate your shoulders and neck. If you aren't already incorporating exercise into your schedule, now is the time to consider it seriously.

BASIC TOOLS

A Good Iron

While it is not uncommon for a home to be without an iron and an ironing board, no quilter is without them. Pressing is the secret when it comes to creating flat, accurate patchwork. Don't worry about getting roped into extra service, however. Just as making quilts does not singularly qualify you to sew on buttons, pressing patchwork is not adequate training for white shirts! For patchwork I prefer a good steam iron and a cotton ironing board cover. Experience has taught me to steer away from reflective-type ironing board covers. I seem more likely to burn my fingers when using them, and I've had several unfortunate experiences with fabric distortion that seemed to go away once I eliminated the reflective cover.

An iron is indispensable not only for pressing fabric and seams, but also for fusing. More and more quilt makers and fabric crafters are finding fusible products helpful. Basically, a "fusible" is an adhesive that can be heat-activated. For a project using fusibles, see the Scrappy Star Wall Hanging (pages 75–77).

Needles

Many machine quilters look forward to using a variety of beautiful threads in their work. You need to be aware that different thread fibers and thicknesses require different needle types and sizes. To avoid frustration it's important not to underestimate the close relationship between needle and thread and to choose both appropriately. Chances are that you don't change your sewing machine needle often enough. Sewing machine needles receive heavy use and wear out fast. For the best results get in the habit of changing the needle with the start of every major project. "If it isn't broken, don't fix it," is a popular adage, but not the proper way to deal with sewing machine needles.

Kinds of Needles The most common needle is a universal, designed for use on both knit and woven fabrics. Others include ballpoint needles (for knits), sharps (for woven fabrics), denim/jeans needles (these are extra-strong sharps), stretch needles, topstitching needles, and double and triple needles. The most recent introduction is the machine embroidery needle, which has a larger eye in relation to the shaft than other machine needles.

Needle Sizes Read your sewing machine manual to find out the proper needle size and type for your machine. While most machines work well with the universal 90/14 or 80/11 needles, there are exceptions. It is especially important to consult your manual if you have a slant-needle or European-made machine. An improper needle can cause irritating mistakes, such as skipped stitches, and can actually damage the machine, usually in the bobbin case area.

The Needle's Eye In addition to needle size, you need to consider the eye of the needle. All size 14 needles have the same-sized shaft, but the width of the point and size of the eye will vary, depending on the kind of needle chosen. For example, a machine embroidery needle will have a larger eye and will accommodate a thicker thread than the same-size sharp needle. Generally, you should choose as small an eye as the thread you are using will allow. Too large a hole created by a large needle will let the bobbin thread pull through or show excessively. You especially want a small needle if you are machine-quilting through fused fabric, when the hole becomes permanent.

Rotary Cutting Systems

This is a book on machine quilting, not piecing, but I still want to give a special plug for rotary cutting systems. The rotary cutter and its accessories have revolutionized the way most quilters cut. The cutter itself looks like a glorified pizza cutter. Because the blade is razor-sharp, a self-healing cutting mat is placed under the fabric to protect the work surface. The small slits that the blade cuts in the mat's surface repair themselves readily, maintaining the mat's usefulness for years. Completing the set is a ¼-inch-thick acrylic ruler, which provides a rigid edge against which to roll the cutter blade. In recent years, the quilting industry has introduced various precut shapes, such as triangles and hexagons, in addition to straightedge rulers.

Rotary cutting systems have several advantages over marking and cutting with scissors. They are extremely effective with multiple layers, increasing the number of pieces you can cut at one time. Because the fabric remains flat while being cut, accuracy is practically guaranteed. There is also less stress on your hand and fingers when doing large amounts of cutting in a short time period.

Many of the projects in this book emphasize the use of a rotary cutting system. If you do not have one, the fabric pieces can, of course, be cut with scissors.

Safety Pins

Using safety pins instead of needle and thread is a handy way to baste quilt layers together. Because you don't have to put one hand underneath the quilt, as you do with thread basting, you avoid distorting the layers. For a full-sized quilt, 350 safety pins is about the minimum you will need. I prefer rustproof nickel safety pins, size 1.

Bicycle Clips

Yes, we are talking about the same clips used to keep wide pant legs from catching in a bike chain. In quilting, bicycle clips are used to secure a quilt that has been rolled and made ready for machine quilting. Clips are optional—very optional—but some people feel they can't machine-quilt without them.

Stencils, Marking Tools, and Light Tables

The machine-quilting techniques I'll be discussing first (Chapters 4 and 5) do not require any knowledge or decisions about marking. We'll pick up marking later on (beginning with Chapter 6), and I'll fill you in on the tools and equipment needed then.

Other Tools for Easy Piecing

Most of the tools you need for machine quilting are probably already in your sewing supplies. Still, if you browse through a quilt shop or visit quilt shows, you will discover that there are people lying awake nights thinking up new tools to make our quilt-making efforts easier, more accurate, more fun, and probably more rewarding. You might consider buying a few.

MATERIALS

Fabric

When selecting fabrics for machine quilting, remember that solid colors tend to look empty if they are not heavily quilted, whereas small, low-contrast prints and textures do not. If you plan to do lots of close quilting, it will show more clearly on plain fabric.

Printed patchwork designs are made to order for beginning machine quilters. Some quilt makers look askance at printed patchwork or appliqué and call it "cheater fabric," but I call it "user-friendly!" It is ideal when you want to practice machine quilting in the early stages, because there is no worry about "ruining" hours of patchwork or appliqué. It also makes for fun, easy, and pretty gifts.

User-friendly fabrics look hand-pieced and hand-appliquéd, but the designs are actually commercially printed. Add batting and backing and you are ready to machine-quilt.

Thread

Cotton and Cotton-Wrapped Polyester For machine piecing, I prefer size 50 100% cotton thread or, as a second choice, cotton-wrapped polyester. To minimize lint in your machine, choose threads that are smooth and without furry edges.

Quilting Thread I am familiar with at least two kinds of thread referred to as "quilting thread." The most common, made by many manufacturers, is treated with a waxlike finish and is intended for hand quilting only. The other, made by Mettler, is size 40 100% cotton mercerized thread, and it is intended for both hand and machine quilting. It is available in many colors. When machine-quilting a solid-color surface, I like to use this quilting thread and match the thread color to the fabric.

Decorative Threads So many wonderful sewing threads are available today that it is easy to become a thread collector. I consider Sulky rayon decorative thread the easiest to use. As I write this, Sulky offers 193 colors in size 40 and 51 in size 30. The selection includes many solid, variegated, and metallic threads, with new colors being added all the time. Other companies offer similar threads, and some manufacture novelty threads and ribbons for sewing. If you begin to do a considerable amount of surface design, you may want to look at yarns, which can be couched in place.

Monofilament Nylon Thread If you were sewing in the 1960s, you might have been tempted to try the newest invisible thread— a thick nylon that resembled cheap fishing line. This is not the same nylon thread quilters are using today. The new thread is more like slightly coarse hair (ask for size 80 or size .004) and comes in two colors, clear and smoky. On the spool, "smoky" looks very dark, causing many people to shy away from using it. In my experience, however, clear monofilament is more reflective and visible than the smoky. I prefer smoky for everything except the very lightest ecrus, pastels, and white fabrics.

On most machines it is necessary to loosen the top tension slightly when using invisible thread. The signal to loosen is a slight drawing up or puckering along the stitching line. Invisible thread is very resilient and will stretch against tight tension in the machine. When you quit stitching, it draws back up just like a rubber band that has been stretched and then relaxed.

The good news is that puckered stitching is easily removed. Examine it closely and you will more than likely find that the bobbin thread has been pulled up through the quilt, showing visible loops on the top side. The nylon thread will be running through the loops, and once you get a good grip on it, you'll be able to pull it right out. If you have stitched over a large area, clip the nylon thread every yard so that you're not drawing out interminable lengths. When you are finished, the bobbin thread will pull out from the underside like chain stitching.

Stories sometimes circulate about nylon thread melting in a dryer or under a hot iron. I have never had a problem using my gas dryer, but I think that electric dryers tend to be hotter and can overdry the clothes. I do not recommend putting a quilt in a hot dryer under any circumstance. If you know you have a very hot dryer or a heavy hand with an iron, be sure to use extra caution on quilts sewn with monofilament thread.

One last word of caution: Always cut and discard loose ends of monofilament thread in a wastebasket, not on the sewing room floor. Stray pieces can wreak havoc with your vacuum cleaner and can prove dangerous for inquisitive children and pets who might ingest them.

Winding an Invisible-Thread Bobbin

When I was first introduced to invisible thread, I was told to use it only as the needle thread, never in the bobbin. Nylon monofilament thread is very springy, and in a full bobbin it tends to unwind and get tangled up in the bobbin mechanism, causing considerable grief. When I began piecing my quilt backs and wanted to have invisible thread in both the top and bobbin of my machine, I learned that I could prevent mishaps by winding the bobbin no more than half full. Even though the thread still tends to spin off, the bobbin case contains it. Don't worry that you'll be winding more bobbins than usual either. Monofilament thread is so fine that a half-filled bobbin generally contains more yardage than a full bobbin of cotton or cotton-wrapped polyester.

Batting

Choosing a Batting No one can decide for you what kind of quilt batting you will like best, and probably no one will change your mind once you do decide. This section provides a brief introduction to the various types of batting available. On the surface, the choice might appear to be a simple one between cotton and polyester, but the batting universe is much more complex. Most quilters, in fact, use different battings for different projects, depending on the technique and fabrics they are using.

If you have not yet developed your own personal batting preferences, my observations are as good a starting place as any. I do recommend that you talk with others who are using the same quilting method as you and that you find out what batting they have tried or why they prefer a particular batting. Beg for scraps that you can use to make sample squares. Test-shrink cotton batting two ways—both before and after quilting—to see which effect you prefer. Get the latest information about batting from salespeople at quilt and fabric stores.

So many new battings are constantly being introduced that I may well have a new favorite by the time you read this. For specific projects you might want to consider an exotic batting made of wool or silk. At the time of this writing, Hobbs was introducing a lovely wool batting for national distribution. You might also discover a batting from a small company with a regional distribution to be perfectly adequate. Remember, this discussion is not meant to be all-inclusive!

- *Bonded Polyester Medium-Weight Batting.* Bonded polyester is my favorite type of batting for minimal machine or hand quilting on bed quilts and for most Quilt-As-You-Sew projects. The fibers are lightweight and easy to care for, and the bonding helps minimize fiber migration. The loft creates a slightly puffy look. For a tied quilt, use the thicker version or layer two regular-weight batts. *Brand names:* Hobbs Poly-down®; Poly-fil Extra-loft®. Many battings sold by the yard from rolls also fit this description.
- *Black Bonded Polyester.* Dark, almost-black battings were developed for dark quilts as a remedy to fiber migration, or bearding. Bearding appears as tiny tufts of batting that have worked their way through the fabric to the surface of the quilt. Beards of white batting on a dark quilt are especially noticeable and detract from the quilt, but dark battings, when they do beard, are much less noticeable. As a bonus, the darker batting seems to intensify dark colors in fabrics. *Brand name:* Hobbs Poly-down Dark.
- *"New-Age" Cotton Batting.* I tacked on the "new-age" label to distinguish this batting from the cotton batting in antique quilts. Until very recently, cotton batting meant lots of quilting—lines of stitching no more than 1 inch apart—to hold the fibers in place and keep them from balling up. Manufacturers of "new-age" cotton battings claim 4 to 8 inches can be left unquilted. Different brands have different shrinkage characteristics, so be sure to read the instructions carefully; some require washing before use. Several are actually 80% cotton and 20% polyester, not 100% cotton.

  Cotton batting generally requires less pinning than polyester because it attracts and holds the cotton quilt top to its surface. As I attempt more complete coverage with machine quilting, I find I am using these "new-age" cotton battings more often. I also like them in garments. They mold to the body shape better than polyester and do not puff, though they are heavier. *Brand names:* Fairfield's Cotton Classic™; Hobbs' Heirloom™; Warm and Natural™ from Warm Products.
- *"Old-Style" Cotton Batting.* Still requested by many hand quilters, "old-style" cotton batting is less dense than the "new-age" type, for a very flat, antique look. Regular Mountain Mist® is more likely to shrink with washing, creating an antique, crinkled look. *Brand name:* Mountain Mist® from Stearns and Foster. There is also a Mountain Mist® Blue Ribbon that isn't as flat as "old-style" or as lofty as "new-age."
- *Very Lightweight Polyester.* Very lightweight polyester is the only polyester batting I currently use in garments. I also like it in small quilts because the flatness seems more in scale and the drape is very soft. Sometimes I layer it on polyester fleece to line cotton toys like dolls and bears that are to be stuffed. The lining helps camouflage any bumps that might appear after stuffing. *Brand name:* Thermore® from Hobbs.
- *Polyester Fleece.* I use polyester fleece to line stuffed cotton toys and pillows, line placemats, and make fabric Christmas ornaments. Fusible fleece is also available, but you can make your

own using standard fleece and a paper-backed fusible web. Attach it using a press cloth, following the manufacturer's directions. *Brand name:* Thermolam® by Stacy.

• *Polyester Fiberfill.* Fiberfill is typically used to stuff pillows, dolls, and other dimensional items. In quilting, loose fiberfill is used in trapunto, even if a cotton batt is being used in the quilt. *Brand names:* Poly-fil® & Poly-fil Supreme®; Poly-down® fiberfill from Hobbs.

Batting Sizes An interesting example of the tail wagging the dog is the way packaged batting is sized. Batting sizes were developed early in this century. They were based on the maximum width of manufacturing equipment and have little to do with popular quilt sizes. Nevertheless, they have become standard in the industry. To compensate, quilt makers must buy up a size—king size for a queen-sized quilt, for example—or else cut some of the batt off the end and sew it on the side, a tedious experience at best. To avoid coming up short when you're making a quilt, jot down the approximate finished size of the quilt and bring your figures along when you shop for batting. Buy a batting that exceeds the finished size in both directions. You can save the parts you trim off for smaller projects.

Saving Leftover Batting

Before rolling leftover batting up and putting it back in the plastic bag, measure what is left and jot down the amount on a piece of paper. If the leftover piece is an odd shape, sketch the shape and add dimensions. Slip the paper inside the bag along with the batting so that your notes are visible through the plastic. If you do much quilting, it won't be long until you have quite an assortment of leftovers. These little notes will save going through endless bags to find the most usable batting later.

4

FEED DOGS UP: HIDDEN QUILT-AS-YOU-SEW

Most people find the easiest way to learn a new technique is to build on information and skills they already have. Since you already know how to sew by machine, the most logical place to start machine quilting is with those techniques that are most like machine garment sewing. That means string quilting.

The first thing you need to know about string piecing and string quilting is there are no strings involved—at least, not the string we might use for flying a kite. *String piecing* is a historic term that refers to the scraps, or "strings," of fabric left over from other projects. The distinction between string piecing and string quilting can be confusing, and the confusion is compounded by the fact that not all quilters use the same vocabulary. Some use the term *stitch and flip* to refer to both techniques. I like to call string quilting *Quilt-As-You-Sew*, but as you will see, it is not the only method in that category.

BASIC STRING PIECING AND STRING QUILTING

Diagram 1

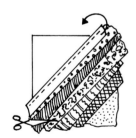

String piecing is stitching fabric scraps of nearly any size or shape to a paper foundation (Diagram 1). This paper foundation can be precut to represent an entire block or any shape you chose. The scraps extend beyond the edge and are trimmed off later.

To begin, two fabric pieces are placed right sides together on the paper foundation. A seam is stitched through all three layers. When the top piece is flipped over, the raw seam edge is covered. New pieces are added in the same way, so that each one conceals the previous raw edge. When the jagged edges are trimmed and the paper is removed, the result is a perfect pieced shape. It will still require quilting.

String quilting sews strips directly onto batting and a fabric backing, instead of onto paper. As you join the fabric pieces together, you are also quilting through the layers. No machine stitching shows on top, but it does show on the backing. When the piecing is completed, so is the quilting.

The String-Quilted Jewelry Travel Case (pages 39–43) is a perfect first project for getting acquainted with string quilting. If you prefer a project without a zipper, just substitute 12½- by 18½-inch rectangles for the rectangular fabric pieces in steps 1 and 2 below. When the string quilting is completed, bind the edges for a set of pretty place mats (see the photo on page 39).

String quilting is easy and fun, and if you have never tried it, I hope you will. It is one of my favorite ways to work with scraps.

Making String-Quilted Fabric

For string quilting, set up your machine with the same thread and stitch length you like for piecing. If you have an even-feed attachment or a built-in even-feed feature on your machine, be sure to use it. If not, watch to make sure the presser foot does not push the topmost layers of fabric and batting further than the bottom layers as you sew. Releasing the pressure on the presser foot may minimize the distortion.

A medium- to low-loft batt is best for the Jewelry Case project. I generally use a medium-loft bonded polyester batting for string-quilted bed quilts and new-age cotton batting for smaller projects.

1. For the Jewelry Case project cut one 8- by 13-inch rectangle and one 3½- by 15-inch rectangle from fabric. (This fabric will appear as the jewelry case lining.) Cut two batting rectangles to match.

2. Lay the fabric pieces right side down and place the batting pieces on top. Pin together at the outside corners. Using a water-erasable marking pen or a dull pencil, draw the jewelry case pattern outline on the larger batting and the side strip on the smaller batting.

3. Work out a piecing plan on paper or practice arranging fabric pieces on the batting, using your drawn outline as a guide. Diagram 2 shows several variations of string-quilted fabric for the jewelry case. The numbers indicate the order in which the strips are positioned. Select one variation to follow or trace the empty shape and create your own. It is a good idea to practice

Diagram 2

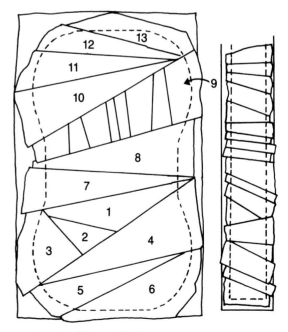

Irregular Strips with Prepiecing

(continued on p. 38)

Diagram 2 *(continued)*

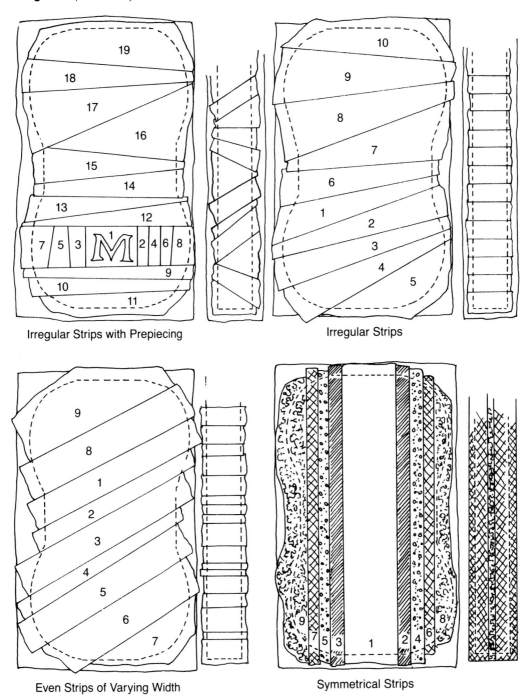

Irregular Strips with Prepiecing

Irregular Strips

Even Strips of Varying Width

Symmetrical Strips

drawing the pieces in order. The challenge is to leave no raw edges exposed inside the drawn outline.

4. Select the first "string" of fabric and position it on the batting. Lay a second "string" right side down on top. Stitch down whichever edge is appropriate, and then flip the top piece over. Proceed until the outline is covered. If you wish you can add machine embroidery, machine-stitched monograms, or small pieces of lace to make the effort even more special.

SIZE

4½ × 6 × 2 inches tall

MATERIALS REQUIRED

8- × 13-inch string-quilted fabric (see earlier)

3½- × 15-inch string-quilted fabric (see earlier)

15-inch square decorative lining fabric

1 yard ⅛-inch piping

14-inch dress zipper

1- × 36-inch bias strip

Additional lining fabric and a small piece of batting will be needed if you wish to make the optional pad for inserting inside the jewelry case.

Figure A

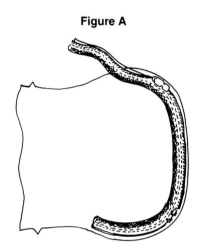

Cutting and Marking the Fabric

1. Using the Jewelry Case pattern (pages 41 and 42), cut the larger piece from string-quilted fabric. Cut one side strip from the remaining string-quilted fabric and one from the lining fabric.
2. Clip into the seam allowance on the string-quilted case to mark the ends of the fold lines (see pattern).
3. Baste along the fold lines to mark them. Accuracy is essential, since these lines will be used as a guide to install the zipper and to sew the case so that it stands straight.

Adding the Piping

1. Place the case right side up and lay the piping around the edge with the raw edges facing out (Figure A). Pin in place so that the piping stitching falls right on the case's ¼-inch seam allowance (this step ensures accuracy in case the piping seam allowance is not an even ¼ inch). Begin and end the piping along the side of the case (not near a fold line).
2. Sew the piping in place using a zipper foot.
3. Clip the piping seam allowance at the fold lines to match the previous clips.

Adding the Zipper

You may not be familiar with this project's method for inserting a zipper, which leaves the zipper teeth completely exposed. Read the instructions thoroughly before beginning. You will see that the zipper is opened and sewn in position one half at a time, beginning with the side strip. The remainder of the zipper is sewn after the side strip is attached to the case.

1. Lay the string-quilted side strip right side up. Open the zipper and lay it face down against one long edge, tape edge aligned with the case edge (Figure B). Lay the lining right side down on top, edge aligned with zipper tape and string-quilted edges. Sew through all layers ¼ inch from edge.
2. Turn the string-quilted fabric and the lining right side out. Press away from the zipper. Baste the opposite long edges together (Figure C).

Figure B

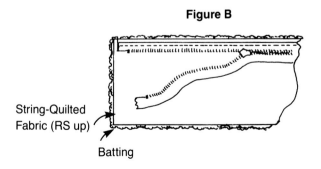

String-Quilted
Fabric (RS up)

Batting

Figure C

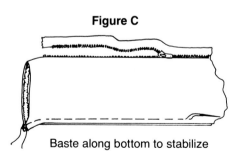

Baste along bottom to stabilize

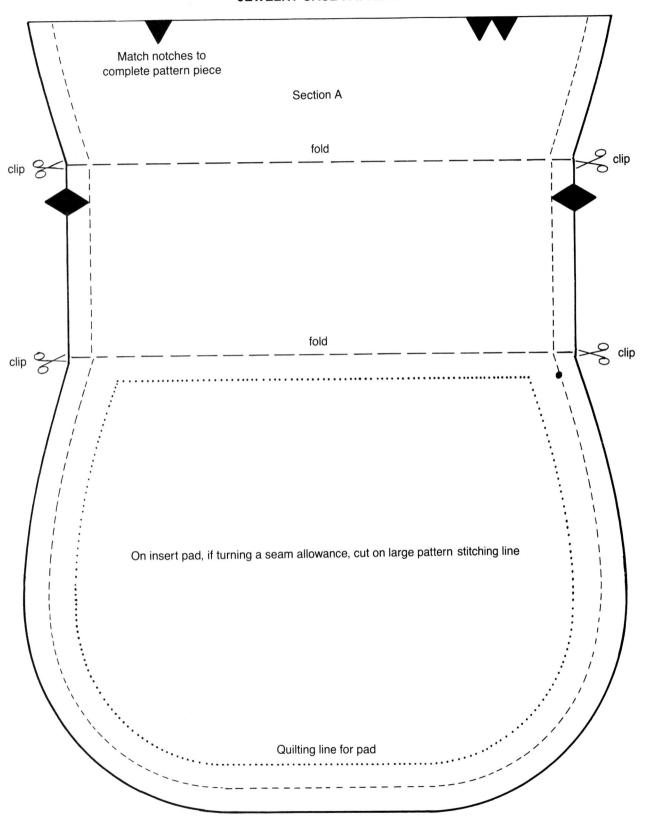

Match notches to
complete pattern piece

Section A

fold

clip

clip

fold

clip

clip

On insert pad, if turning a seam allowance, cut on large pattern stitching line

Quilting line for pad

B

A

Assembly Diagram

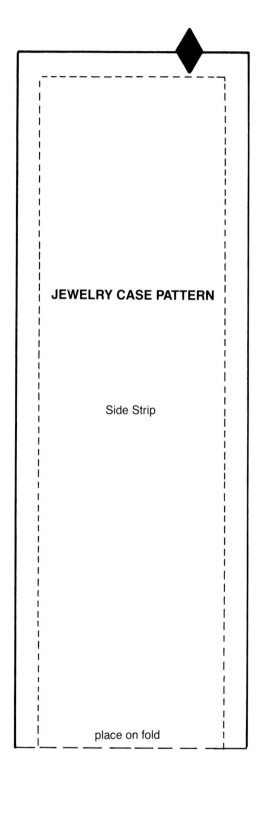

JEWELRY CASE PATTERN

Side Strip

place on fold

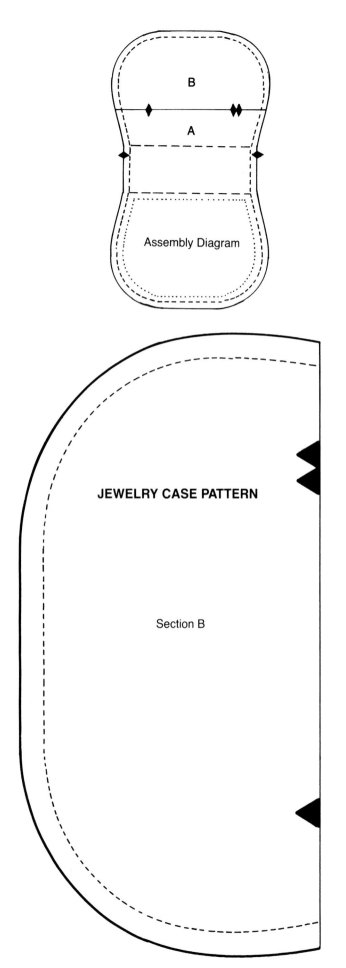

JEWELRY CASE PATTERN

Section B

Attaching the Side Panel and Completing the Zipper

1. Sew the side panel to the bottom of the case as follows: Beginning with one short end, match the single notches in the panel to those on the case, right sides facing, and pin in position (Figure D). Sew around the bottom and up the sides, leaving the zipper edge (the top of the case) open.

2. Working from both ends toward the middle, pin the free zipper half to the top of the case. Ease to fit, matching the zipper tape to the raw edges. The metal zipper stop should match the dot on the pattern. Check to make sure the case folds smoothly on the basted lines and stands straight; adjust as necessary. Sew the zipper in position and cut off the tape ends even with the fold lines.

3. Trim the batting out of the seam allowances.

Finishing the Jewelry Case

For a professional finish, all the interior exposed seam allowances are covered with a 1- by 36-inch bias strip.

1. Place the bias strip against the exposed seam allowance, fold down the end, and pin (Figure E). Stitch in place all around.

2. Fold the strip over the seam allowance, fold the raw edge under, and slip-stitch, concealing the previous stitching (Figure F).

Figure D

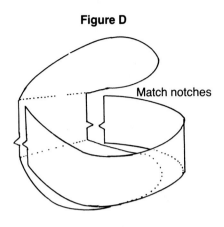

Match notches

Figure E

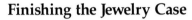

Figure F

Making the Inside Pad

A pad inside the jewelry case can hold pins or divide pieces of jewelry to keep them from getting tangled. You may want more than one. The pad pattern is marked on the case pattern. The same pattern can be used to cut plastic canvas for pierced earring storage.

1. Cut two pads from fabric and one from batting.

2. Place the fabric pieces right sides facing and layer the batting on top. Sew all around, leaving an opening along the straight edge for turning. Clip seam allowances along curves.

3. Turn the pad right side out, and slip-stitch the opening closed.

FABULOUS FIRST MACHINE QUILT

Diagram 3

Some years ago I judged a contest to find great-looking, but quick, quilting ideas. The winner in the full-sized quilt category was Carolee Knutson from Ames, Iowa, with a string-quilted quilt in red and yellow calico strips that looked something like Diagram 3. She made the quilt for her son to take to college, and the fabrics represented his school colors, cardinal and gold. I never saw the quilt or the idea again, but as I was preparing this book it came to mind as one of the easiest first quilts ever. The string-quilting technique introduced in the jewelry case project is one of the easiest methods of Quilt-As-You-Sew, so why not make a whole quilt that way? That was exactly what Carolee had done.

I explained the winning quilt, as I remembered it, to Ellen Rosintoski, who teaches machine quilting in her own right, but also helps out in my studio. She made a pink and blue crib quilt for me (see below). Then she said, "What a great idea! It is so easily adapted to any size, mood, or color scheme, why not have a class and see what other people do?" She put a little notice for a mystery class in the quilt guild newsletter, and six people responded. By the time the class day rolled around, I had found some bear fabric and had talked Ellen into making a second crib quilt. Ellen gave general instructions to the class, showed the two crib quilts as examples, and said they could use any fabric they wanted and make any variation on the basic design.

Take a look at the amazing variety of quilts this small class produced; then follow the basic Bears Crib Quilt instructions (pages 49–51) to make your own version.

Quilts from Ellen's Class

The farm quilt came from my studio, with most of the sewing done by Martha Dudley. Having been raised on a farm, I'm always drawn to farm fabrics, and this year there was a bumper crop! The quilt is a good example of how a group of fabrics with a single theme can work together. The large print reduces the amount of string quilting and sets the theme at the same time. Some meandering free-motion quilting with invisible thread (p. 108) was added to the large print.

Betty Alvarez gets the prize for the most elegant, not to mention biggest, quilt. It incorporates a wonderful collection of gold-embellished fabrics spread over six 20-inch panels. Partway through the first panel, Betty decided a 45-degree angle was too extreme for the king size and she started over at 30 degrees.

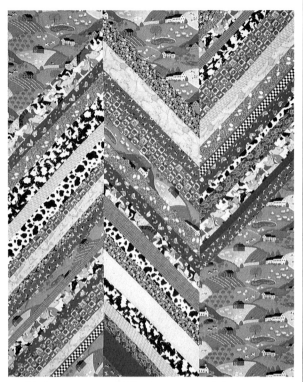

Sue Carter had been planning to make quilts for twin beds and decided this would be a good design, since the quilts could be similar and compatible without having to be identical. She worked out a simple design in Amish colors, but once the first quilt was assembled, she decided it needed considerably more quilting to look right. She is adding lots of machine quilting and some hand quilting. The quilts are wonderful but did not retain the original benefit of quick and easy.

Sandy Henry wasn't able to come to class, so she just followed the instructions. She remembered Ellen saying, "Make something bright and cheery." Sandy must have one of the best collections of bright and cheery fabric ever assembled. She completely covered all four panels of a queen/double quilt with eye-popping colors. No large sections of one fabric and the sharp 45-degree angle give this quilt a strong dimensional look.

Micheline Prescott also decided to quilt for her son. Ishon, who is eleven, picked out the "jammin" background fabric himself. Having seen and liked Betty's quilt, Micheline used the same 30-degree angle for her strips. Afterward she felt that 45 degrees might have been better because of the high-contrast colors and the limited number of strips.

Sammy Simpson jumped ahead. She asked if it was all right to cut the strips into smaller pieces. She cut each strip into four squares, then string-quilted across each square. By alternating the direction of every other square, she created larger, interlocking concentric squares. Her quilt is the perfect transition to our next technique, Quilting by the Block (p. 51).

Claudia Litton wanted to make a patriotic quilt for her son Andy, because, as she says, "He loves America." Sue found dachshund fabric in memory of Scooter, his pet of twelve years, and added appliqués to represent two new dogs, Muffy and Buffy, and a cat, Dutch. Other fabrics represent his golf hobby and Christmas, his favorite holiday. Patchwork practice squares lined up in rows add interest. Most of the class quilts have themes, but this is the most personal quilt in the group—and Claudia's first full-sized quilt! Andy loves the quilt and has named it "American Life."

Bears Crib Quilt

Fabric Selection

String quilting makes an ideal showcase for large prints that get lost when cut for the typical quilt block. Let one large print set the theme for the whole quilt. Generally, the quilt is most effective when it is made with a scrap quilt look, which requires a little bit of lots of different fabrics. Select them with variety in mind, but relate them to the theme fabric.

Preparing the Backing and Batting

1. For the Bears Crib Quilt as photographed cut three 14-inch-wide panels of backing fabric 54 inches long, or approximately 3 inches longer than the desired finished length of the quilt top.

   If you are making a larger quilt, cut the backing panel half the width of the fabric (about 22 inches) and use three panels for a twin quilt, four for a queen/double, or five for a king size. See the pictures of additional quilts (pages 45–47).

2. Cut the batting 1 inch larger all around than the backing panel.

3. Fold the backing in half and mark the center. On the right side of the fabric, mark a 45-degree line approximately in the center of the panel (Figure A). A quilt such as the Bears requires that you think about which direction the fabric strips are going. Be sure to mark panels accordingly if the design planned requires the quilting lines to chevron.

4. Place the batting on a flat surface and lay the backing fabric on top, right side up. Hold the two layers in place with safety pins.

5. Using thread that matches the backing fabric, sew along the marked line through the backing and batting. Use a walking foot with the sewing machine if available. This seam line will be used to establish the correct angle for the strips, in addition to keeping the batting and backing in place.

Preparing the Fabric Strips

Strips must be a minimum of 21 inches long if using 14-inch-wide backing strips. Lengths at least 23 inches long work best. If you are using 22-inch-wide backing strips, use 35-inch lengths. Most people are surprised by how long these strips need to be.

Cut strips on the straight grain of the fabric, lengthwise or crosswise, depending upon the design and your preference. The number of strips needed depends upon the widths they are cut, as well as on the width of the accent fabric, if one is used.

To achieve the scrappy look cut strips in widths varying from 1¾ inches to 4 inches. Add interest to the strips by piecing a few from strip sets or using Seminole piecing.

If you choose to accent a special fabric, cut this strip at least 18 inches long by 25 inches wide. If the fabric has a directional design like the bear print that you want to keep upright, the accent strip should be cut with a 45-degree angle at the top and bottom (Figure B).

SIZE
41 × 54 inches

MATERIALS REQUIRED
1½ yards of backing fabric
1½ yards of batting
1½ yards of accent fabric
3 yards of assorted scraps for quilt top
¼ yard of fabric for finishing strips, cut crosswise and pieced
¼ yard of fabric for flap border, cut crosswise and pieced
½ yard of fabric for second border, cut crosswise and pieced
⅝ yard of fabric for French-fold binding

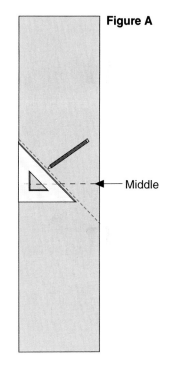

Figure A

Middle

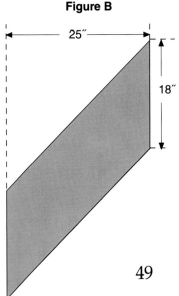

Figure B

25″

18″

49

Sewing the Individual Quilt Panels

1. If there is an accent strip, like the bears, it is the first piece, whether it will be used in the center, top, or bottom of the quilt panel. Place the accent strip right side up on top of the batting, and pin in place.

    If there is no specific accent strip, but a more random look, it is easier to start in the middle and work in both directions. Place the first strip right side up.

2. Select the strips that will go above and below the accent strip. Place these strips face down on top of the accent strip, raw edges even (Figure C). Check each strip carefully to be sure that it will extend to the edges of the backing after it is sewn and flipped. Pin the strips in place and sew with a ¼-inch seam. Flip each strip so that the raw edge of the seam is covered and the right side of the fabric is up. Press lightly.

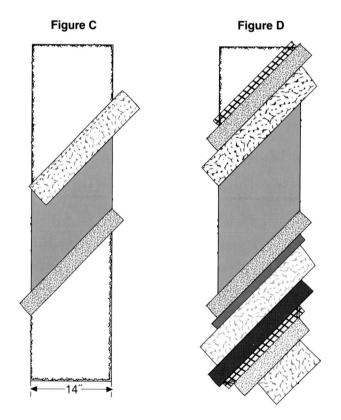

Figure C   **Figure D**

14"

3. Continue adding strips in the same manner, varying strip width and color (Figure D). It is not necessary to trim off ragged ends as you go. It is easier to trim all the edges at one time.

    As you continue to add strips, it is easy to get disoriented and discouraged because the strip ends appear jagged and the panel may begin to look skewed. Remember that the panel top will be trimmed to fit the rectangular backing fabric after all the panels are complete.

4. Make as many panels as necessary for the desired quilt size.

5. After completing all the panels, square the corners and trim the edges to make all the panels the same size.

Assembling the Quilt

Perhaps you've been wondering how to sew these layered panels together without having exposed, messy-looking raw edges. You're right; it can't be a simple seam. The simple solution is finishing strips that are added as the panels are joined. This technique covers the seam allowances that would otherwise show on the back of the quilt.

1. Arrange the quilt panels as desired.
2. The finishing strips are cut on grain 1½ inches wide by 56 inches long, or approximately 2 inches longer than the lengths of the panels to be joined. Cut one less strip than the number of panels to be joined. Press the strips in half lengthwise, wrong sides together.
3. Layer two adjacent panels, right sides facing, and place a folded strip on the panels, aligning all raw edges. Pin the panels and strip together, and stitch ¼ inch from the raw edges through all eight layers (Figure E).
4. Trim away the excess batting in the seam allowance. If the panels are pulled firmly over your knee, the seam opens up and it is easy to trim away the excess batting between the layers of fabric. It is not necessary to cut away fabric.
5. After trimming the batting, press the strip to the side so that it covers all the raw edges. Hand-stitch the folded edge in place with a hidden stitch. If you are clever with your sewing machine and don't mind a machine stitch showing on the finishing strip, this step can be done with your machine hemming stitch.
6. Join the remaining panels in the same manner.
7. The beauty of the technique is that the quilting was done as you added the strips. If you have used an extra-wide accent fabric, you may choose to add surface quilting in that area. This would be a great place to practice the meandering free-motion quilting (page 108).

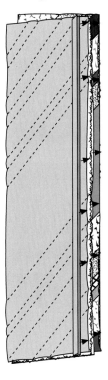

Figure E

Adding the Borders Quilt-As-You-Sew

The Bears Crib Quilt seemed to need a border. The 1¼-inch finished border (1¾-inch cut) was added using the Modified Quilt-As-You-Sew technique on page 196. The border strip on each side is actually covering the ends of diagonal strips. In addition, this quilt features a ¼-inch flap border. (See the discussion of flaps on pages 191–192.)

The actual border is cut on the bias, but only because the check print looked wonderful when it was cut on the bias, not because it needed to be cut on the bias to work.

Finishing the Quilt

The quilt is finished with a ⅜-inch French-fold binding. (Refer to page 198.)

BY THE BLOCK

Creating a specific, repetitive pattern using basic string quilting can be tricky. It is a real treat to discover a traditional quilt block that you can make up using hidden Quilt-As-You-Sew techniques. Virginia Reel and Log Cabin are two block designs that are easily adapted to this style. Generally, you have to look for designs that are pieced from the center out or diagonally, beginning at one corner.

Virginia Reel Quilt

Selecting Fabrics and Batting

The quilt shown has ten light and twenty dark fabrics. It would also be very attractive with ten light and ten dark fabrics. Mix those fabrics and you can still have twenty different combinations. You could even select one light fabric and one dark fabric, but I think the block is too large to use only two fabrics in the entire quilt.

Because there is minimal quilting on these quilts, for batting I prefer the medium-loft, bonded-polyester, or the new-age cotton batts.

SIZE
85 × 101 inches
Block Size: 16 inches square

MATERIALS REQUIRED
½ yard (or 18- × 32-inch scrap) each of 20 assorted dark prints (includes backing for squares)
½ yard each of 10 assorted light prints
⅞ yard of fabric for finishing strips
7½ yards batting
3⅜ yards of backing for borders
⅞ yard of turquoise fabric for first border and corner blocks
⅞ yard of brown fabric for second border
1¾ yards of turquoise and brown print fabric for third border
⅝ yard fabric for French-fold binding

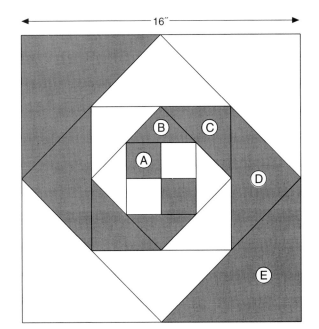

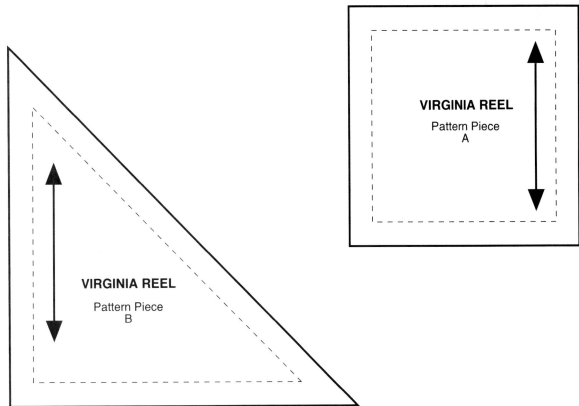

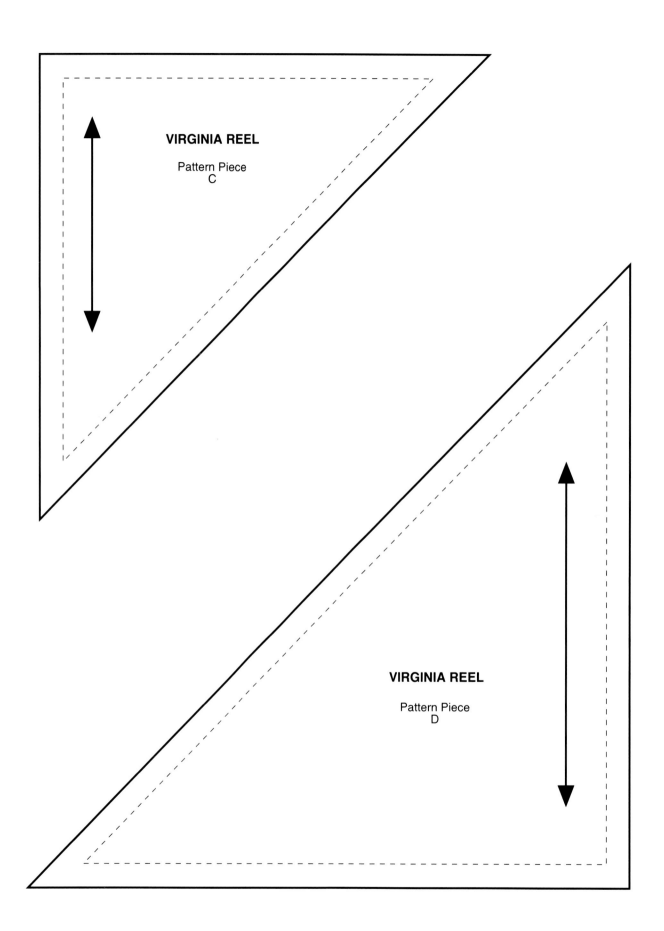

VIRGINIA REEL

Pattern Piece
C

VIRGINIA REEL

Pattern Piece
D

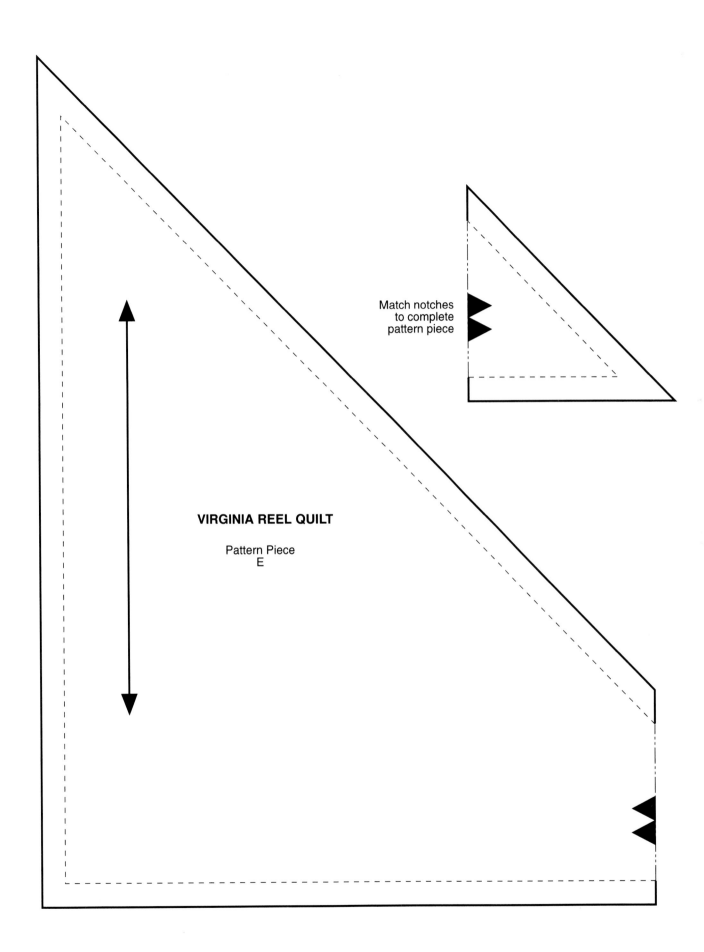

VIRGINIA REEL QUILT

Pattern Piece
E

Match notches
to complete
pattern piece

Cutting the Fabric

A cutting layout is included for layering each light and dark pair of fabrics and cutting with a rotary cutter (Figures A, A-1, A-2).

If you prefer to cut the fabric traditionally, divide and layer the fabric as in the following steps 1 and 2. Use the pattern pieces (pages 53–55), position as shown on the cutting layout, and cut using your scissors (Figures A, A-1, A-2).

Figure A

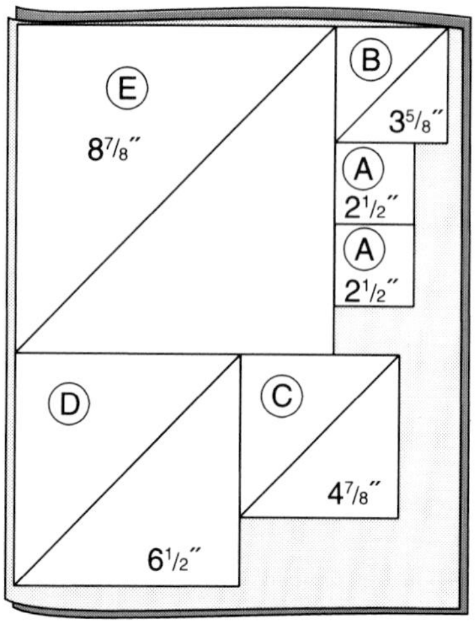

Figure A-1

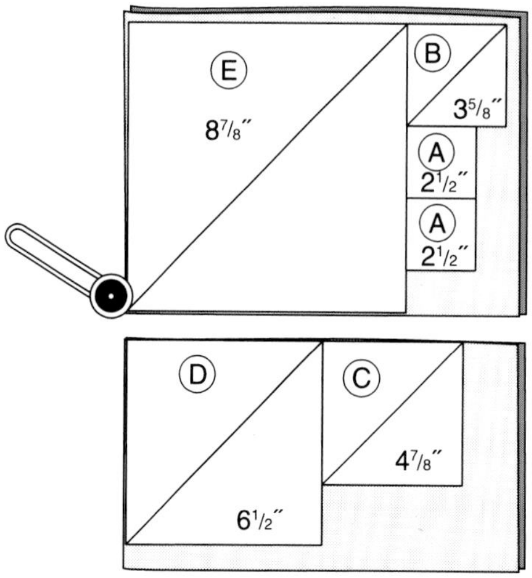

Figure A-2

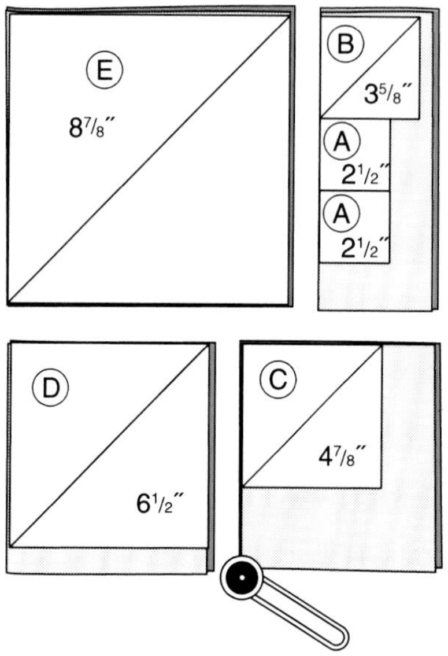

1. Each light fabric will be used for two blocks; from each ½ yard cut two sections 14 inches wide by 18 inches long.
2. From each ½ yard of dark fabric, cut one panel 14 inches wide by 18 inches long, and one 17½-inch square for backing fabric.
3. Sort the proper light and dark 14- by 18-inch fabric pairs for the twenty blocks. Layer each pair with right sides facing, grain lines matching, and all raw edges carefully aligned. Use a rotary cutter and acrylic ruler to measure and cut the fabric (Figure A).

   Cut Squares B, C, D, and E in half diagonally to make two triangles from each square. As shown in Figures A-1 and A-2, when cutting various-sized pieces from one shape, try to make cuts that go all the way across progressively smaller pieces.
4. Cut twenty 17-inch squares of batting. The finished size of the block is 16 inches; the blocks will be trimmed to 16½ inches before they are joined.

Cutting Batting with a Rotary Cutter

A rotary cutter makes a nice, clean cut on batting and is easy to use. The problem is that the fibers from polyester batting seem to be forced into the mat by the blade. The result is a slightly furry mat. My solution is to use one of my old mats exclusively for cutting batting squares. If you don't have the luxury of an old mat, you can reserve the second side of your mat for batting only.

Piecing the Center Square Subunit

When you are new to the Quilt-As-You-Sew technique, it is a good idea to finish one block completely before converting to an assembly-line method.

Choose the first pair of light and dark fabrics. Machine-piece four small A Squares, alternating light and dark fabrics. Keep the fabrics in the same position (Figure B). Press seams toward the dark fabric on the pairs and up on the set of four.

Figure B

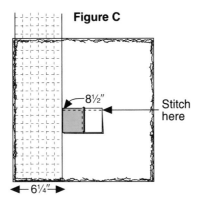

Assembling the Block Quilt-As-You-Sew

1. Layer the backing fabric, wrong side up, with the batting. Fold the prepieced center square in half so that the wrong side of a dark square shows on the left side and the last seam allowance stands up. Place the folded subunit on top of the batting so that the seam line is exactly centered horizontally (8½ inches from top and bottom) along the crosswise grain of the backing fabric and the sides of the pieced square are 6¼ inches from the sides of the batting square (Figure C).

2. Machine-stitch the pieced center square through all four layers on the original horizontal seam line. Flip the top layer of the square up and finger-press.

Figure C

8½"

Stitch here

6¼"

Finger Pressing

Finger pressing is adequate on most Quilt-As-You-Sew steps. If you want to press with the iron, use steam, keep the iron slightly above the surface of the fabric, and let just the point of the iron run along the seam. Reducing the temperature of the iron will prevent polyester batting from melting, should the iron accidentally touch it.

Figure D

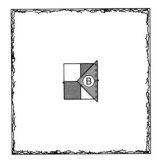

Figure E

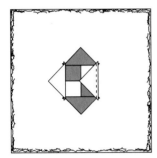

Figure F

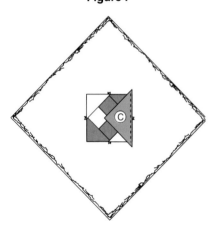

Figure G

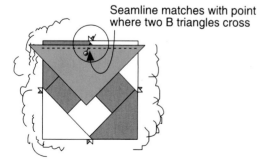

Seamline matches with point where two B triangles cross

Machine-stitch, preferably with monofilament nylon invisible thread, "in the ditch" on the remaining original vertical seam line and through the batting and backing. ("In the ditch" means the space between the two pieces.) To exaggerate the space available, put a slight bit of tension on the seam line. The in-the-ditch stitch is best done with invisible thread. It can be done on all the remaining blocks at one time to reduce the number of times the thread is changed.

3. Position the center square subunit so that a light square is in the upper left corner. Beginning with a Triangle B from dark fabric, place the triangle right side down along the edge of the subunit (Figure D).

Check for clues that the pieces are aligned correctly. The hypotenuse of the triangle should be aligned with the edge of the pieced subunit. The outside corners will extend slightly beyond the outside edges of the subunit. The right-angle point of the triangle should lie along the center seam line of the squares for all Triangles B (and D, in subsequent steps).

Sew the triangle in position. Open out and finger-press.

4. Sew the remaining Triangle B from dark fabric to the opposite edge of the subunit. Rotate the subunit one-quarter turn and sew the two Triangles B from light fabric to the remaining edges in the same manner (Figure E).

5. Rotate the block one-eighth turn clockwise, so that a light triangle is in the upper left corner. Beginning with a Triangle C from dark fabric, place the triangle right side down along the edge of the subunit (Figure F).

Again, check for clues that the pieces are aligned correctly. The short sides of the triangle should extend approximately ¼ inch beyond the interior seams of the center square subunit for all Triangles C (and E, in subsequent steps). For perfect intersections it may be necessary to compromise. Match the ¼-inch seam line on the triangle being added with the point where the two previous triangles cross (Figure G). The raw edge of the new triangle should be parallel to the sewn edge of the previous triangles.

Stitch ¼ inch from the edge of the new triangle. Open out and finger-press. Add the remaining Triangle C from dark fabric and the two Triangles C from light fabric, in the same order as above.

6. With each remaining set of triangles rotate the block to begin with a dark triangle in the upper left corner and add triangles in the same order as above. See the block assembly figure (Figure H).

7. Complete all twenty blocks in the same way.

Figure H

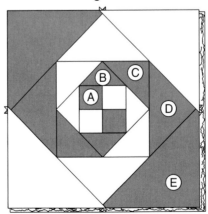

Joining the Blocks into Rows

1. Trim the blocks to 16½ inches square, which includes two ¼-inch seam allowances. This is most easily done with a large square acrylic ruler and the rotary cutter.

2. To eliminate some of the extra bulk the Quilt-As-You-Sew method creates, cut batting approximately ⅜ inch square out of each corner of each block (Figure I). Don't cut backing or design fabric; cut only the batting!

3. Lay out the blocks in five horizontal rows of four blocks each, carefully checking the orientation of the design (see the completed quilt layout). When you are satisfied with the arrangement, it is a good idea to pin a position note, such as Row 1, Block A, on each block (Figure J). Because the orientation of these blocks is crucial, pinning the note in the same corner of each block will provide a double-check as blocks are assembled.

Figure I

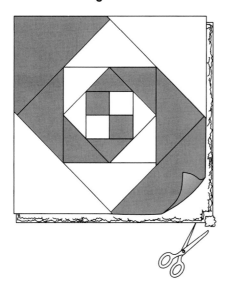

Figure J

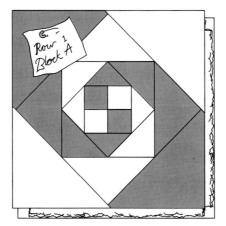

Quilt-As-You-Sew Block Assembly with Finishing Strips

The blocks will be assembled with finishing strips, similar to the long strips used to assemble the panels for the Bears Crib Quilt on page 51. There are some differences here, because finishing strips will be used both vertically, to join the blocks, and horizontally, to join the rows.

1. Cut finishing strips on the lengthwise grain 1½ inches wide and about 18 inches long (approximately 1½ inches longer than the length of the blocks to be joined). Press the strips in half lengthwise with wrong sides facing. The strips can all be cut from the same fabric or from assorted fabrics.

2. Lay two adjacent blocks with their right sides facing. Place a folded strip along the seam line, raw edges even with the block edge. Pin blocks and strip together (Figure K). Stitch ¼ inch from the edge through all eight layers. See Alternating or Aligned Finishing Strips to decide on which block to place the strip.

Figure K

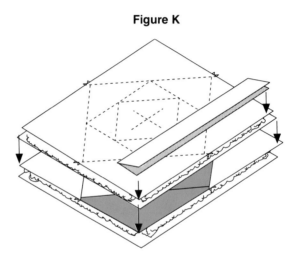

3. Trim out excess batting from the seam allowance, press the strip so that it covers the raw edges, and hand-stitch in place (Figure L). If you are clever with your sewing machine and don't mind the stitch showing on the finishing strip, this step can be done with your machine hemming stitch.

Figure L

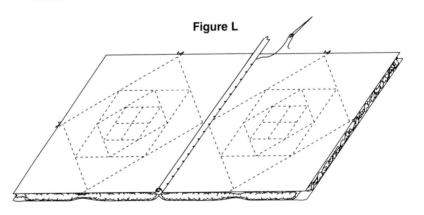

Alternating or Aligned Finishing Strips

The finishing strip actually goes from the seam line approximately ½ inch onto the block it was not touching when the seam was sewn. If you want the strips to alternate from row to row—which reduces bulk at the intersection of four blocks—then practice alternate positioning. On Row 1 all of the strips lie on the block that will be to the left, on Row 2 they lie on the block that will be to the right, on Row 3 it will be back to the left, and so on.

Sometimes it is fun to line up the strips and make a continuous contrasting grid on the back of the quilt. In that case, all strips should be placed consistently on the block that will be to the right all the way through. Or they will be placed consistently on the block that will be to the left.

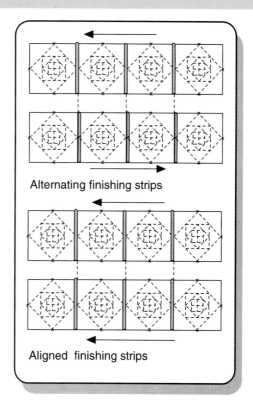

Alternating finishing strips

Aligned finishing strips

Joining the Rows

Once the horizontal rows are completed, assemble them in the same way (Figure M). Cut finishing strips 1½ inches wide by approximately 2 inches longer than the length of the rows to be joined. Line up the block seams carefully before adding the finishing strip. Stitch, trim away excess batting, press the finishing strip flat, and stitch in place.

When the quilt interior is completed, it should measure 64½ by 80½ inches, including ¼-inch seam allowances.

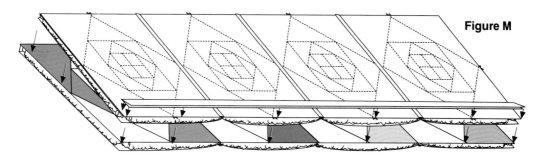

Figure M

Adding the Borders

The borders for this quilt are 2 inches, 2 inches, and 6 inches wide finished. The borders are attached by the standard Quilt-As-You-Sew method. (Please refer to pages 193–195.) The second and third borders are accented with corner blocks (Figure N). (See page 196, Adding a Quilt-As-You-Sew Border with Corner Blocks.)

Finishing the Quilt

A ⅝-inch French-fold binding finishes the quilt. (Please refer to page 198 for details.)

Foundation Piecing

As this book is going to press there is a buzz in the quilt world about foundation piecing, especially in miniature-sized blocks. Some people are marketing printed paper; others sell rubber stamps for you to stamp either paper or fabric foundations. The point is that nearly all of the designs that can be pieced that way can be converted to full-sized hidden Quilt-As-You-Sew quilt blocks.

Virginia Reel Wall Hanging

SIZE

58 × 58 inches
Block Size: 11¼ inches square

MATERIALS REQUIRED

⅜ yard each of 16 assorted blue fabrics
   (includes backing for squares)
1½ yards of white fabric
4 yards batting
1¾ yards backing for borders
⅝ yard blue print fabric for first border
¾ yard blue fabric for second border
¾ yard blue print fabric for third
   border
⅝ yard for French-fold binding

The Virginia Reel Wall Hanging variation is made using the same quilt-by-the-block techniques as the full-sized quilt. You will need to read those instructions (pages 53–62) if you have not already done so. The quilt block is made smaller and more suitable for a wall hanging by eliminating pattern piece E and replacing pattern A with two new pieces (A1 and X), shown in the Wall Hanging Block.

Cutting the Light Fabric

Because the same light fabric is used in every square, the cutting instructions for the light fabric feature quick-cutting strip techniques. Use a rotary cutter to cut strips of fabric, and cut across the strips to make squares. Squares may be cut diagonally to make triangles.

1. For Squares X, cut four 2-inch-wide strips of fabric, each approximately 18 inches long. Cut thirty-two 2-inch squares.
2. For Triangle A1, cut three 2⅞-inch-wide strips of fabric, each approximately 18 inches long. Cut sixteen 2⅞-inch squares. Cut each square in half diagonally to make thirty-two triangles.
3. For Triangle B, cut four strips of fabric 3⅝ inches wide by 18 inches long. Cut sixteen 3⅝-inch squares. Cut squares in half diagonally to make thirty-two triangles.
4. For Triangle C, cut three strips of fabric 4⅞ inches wide by 32 inches long. Cut sixteen 4⅞-inch squares. Cut each square in half diagonally to make thirty-two triangles.
5. For Triangle D, cut four strips of fabric 6½ inches wide by 30 inches long. Cut sixteen 6½-inch squares. Cut each square in half diagonally to make thirty-two triangles.

Virginia Reel Wall Hanging Block

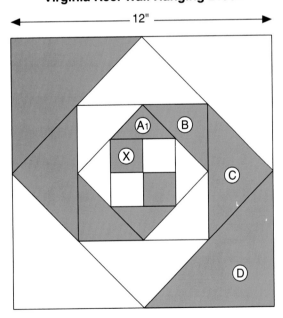

VIRGINIA REEL WALL HANGING

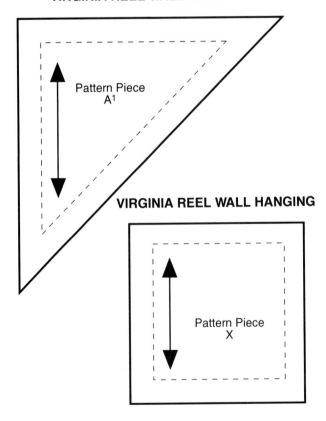

Cutting the Blue Fabric and Batting

The assorted blue fabrics may be layered and cut with a rotary cutter.

1. From each blue fabric, cut a panel 20 inches wide by 8 inches long.
2. Layer up to six panels of blue fabric together, matching grain lines and aligning raw edges carefully. Cut the fabric (Figure A).
3. From the backing fabric, cut sixteen 12¾-inch squares for block backing. Cut sixteen 12¾-inch squares of batting. The finished size of the block is 11¼ inches; the blocks will be trimmed to 11¾ inches before they are joined.

Making the Quilt Block

The center square subunit is assembled in the same manner as for the full-sized quilt (page 57).

When placing the folded center square subunit on top of the batting and centering the seam line horizontally (Figure C from full-sized quilt instructions, page 57), the seam line should be 6⅜ inches from top and bottom, along the crosswise grain of the backing fabric. The sides of the subunit are 4⅝ inches from the sides of the batting square.

Continue as for the full-sized quilt, completing sixteen quilt blocks.

Joining the Blocks into Rows

1. Trim the blocks to 11¾ inches square.
2. Trim a ⅜-inch square of batting out of each corner of each block (Figure I, p. 59, from full-sized quilt instructions).
3. Lay out the blocks in four horizontal rows of four blocks each, carefully checking the orientation of the design. See the completed wall hanging layout (Figure B).
4. Use finishing strips to join the blocks into rows. Cut strips on the lengthwise grain, 1½ inches wide by 13¼ inches long. Refer to Joining the Blocks into Rows from the full-sized quilt instructions on page 59.

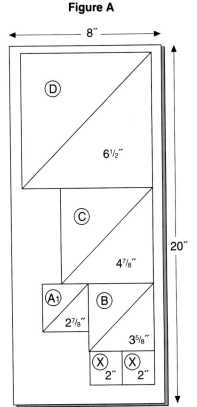

Figure A

Figure B

Joining the Rows

Join the rows together in the same manner as for the full-sized quilt.

Adding the Borders

The borders for this quilt finish to 1¾ inches, 1¼ inches, and 3 inches and are added by the standard Quilt-As-You-Sew method. (Refer to pages 193–195.)

Finishing the Quilt

A ½-inch French-fold binding finishes the quilt. (Refer to page 198 for details.)

Courthouse Steps

The Log Cabin block is probably the world's favorite quilt-as-you-sew block. I covered the subject thoroughly with specific instructions in my *Scrap Patchwork and Quilting* (New York: Meredith Press, 1992). In a traditional Log Cabin block (Figure A-1) the strips spiral out from a center square, creating a block that is divided diagonally into dark and light halves. For this book I chose Courthouse Steps (Figure A-2), a variation also constructed from the center of the block out. Here the strips are added to opposite sides of the center square to create two light and two dark sections.

SIZE

91 × 107 inches
Block Size: 16 inches square

MATERIALS REQUIRED

Thirty 4½-inch square printed designs or motifs for block centers
2¼ yards each of two different ecru fabrics
1½ yards each of two different blue fabrics
1½ yards each of two different red fabrics
9⅛ yards of fabric for backing OR 4⅝ yards of two different fabrics
9⅛ yards of batting, or king size packaged batting
2¾ yards of fabric for border
⅝ yard of fabric for French-fold binding

Figure A-1

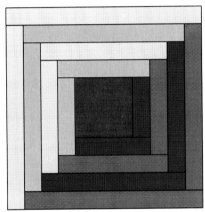

Traditional Log Cabin

Figure A-2

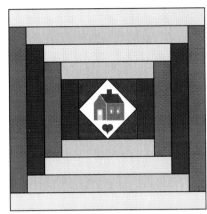

Courthouse Steps

Figure B-2

For ecru 2: Each strip is cut 2″ × 27″. From each strip, sew and trim either (1) 11″ and (1) 14″ strip, or (1) 8″ and (1) 17″ strip.

Figure B-1

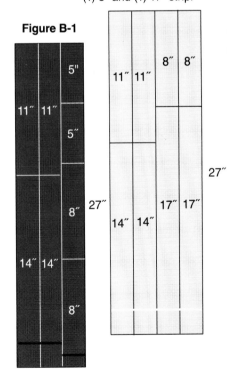

For ecru 1: Each strip is cut 2″ × 27″. From each strip, sew and trim either (1) 11″ and (1) 14″ strip, or (2) 5″ and (2) 8″ strips.

Fabric Selection

The center square of this Courthouse Steps block is 4½ inches cut. This size is large enough to utilize many printed motifs in their entirety, as shown in the four-block photograph. It is probably too large to use a solid-color fabric, but a large print or plaid should also look good.

To make as shown, select two different but similar fabrics for both light and dark sections of each block. The strips are cut wide enough that using only one small print would be boring. The sample layout of blocks alternates red and blue fabrics as the dark color. The crucial decision that makes this particular Courthouse Steps layout work is that the dark colors (red or blue) alternate positions in adjoining blocks. In Block A, made with red and ecru fabrics, the ecru strips are added to the sides and the reds to the top and bottom edges. Block B is made with blues and ecru; the blues are added to the sides and the ecru strips to the top and bottom edges. Note that within each ecru and blue/red section, dark and light shades of the color alternate as well. See Figures D and E and the full quilt diagram, Figure G.

Cutting the Fabric

1. For easier handling and less fraying, cut the strips on the lengthwise grain of the fabric. Use a rotary cutting system to quick-cut 2-inch-wide strips from both the light and dark fabrics. Although some people cut each strip for each block to the exact length required, stitching long strips in place and trimming to the proper length after sewing is generally faster.

Cutting a total of thirty pieces of each length, cut strips from ecru 1 (Figure B-1) and ecru 2 (Figure B-2). From 2-inch-wide strips of red 1 and blue 2, cut thirty 8-inch and thirty 14-inch lengths of each color.

Figure C-1

Stitch and trim

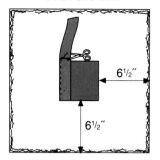

Square is centered on top of batting and backing. Place first ecru strip right side down on left side of center square. Stitch. Trim to size.

Figure C-2

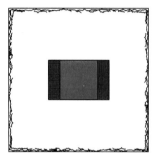

Add second strip to right side of center square, trim, and flip open.

From 2-inch-wide strips of red 2, cut thirty 11-inch and thirty 17-inch lengths; from blue 1, cut thirty 5-inch and thirty 11-inch lengths.

2. Cut thirty 4½-inch center squares.
3. Cut thirty 17½-inch squares each of batting and backing fabric. If you choose two different backing fabrics for Blocks A and B, the back of your assembled quilt will have a checkerboard appearance. The blocks will be trimmed to 16½ inches before they are joined. The finished size of the block is 16 inches.

Making Block A

1. Layer the backing fabric, wrong side up, with the batting on top. Place the 4½-inch center square right side up, so that it is exactly centered on top of the batting (Figure C-1). The edges of the center square should be 6½ inches from each edge of the batting. Use pins through all layers to hold the center square in place.

2. Place the first 5-inch ecru strip right side down on the left side of the center square, aligning raw edges. Sew the strip in position through all four layers. Trim excess length and press open.

   Sew the second strip of this matching ecru pair to the right side of the center square (Figure C-2). Trim and press.

3. Sew the second pair of matching (red) strips to the top and bottom sides of the center square, according to the assembly diagram (Figure D). Trim and press.

4. The third pair of matching strips is the alternate ecru fabric, sewn to the left and right sides of the block.

5. The fourth pair of matching strips is the alternate red fabric, sewn to the top and bottom sides of the block.

6. Continue adding pairs of strips around the block according to Figure D.

7. Complete fifteen A blocks in the same manner.

Making Block B

Block B is assembled in the same manner as Block A, except that the first pair of matching strips to be sewn to the center square is blue. Blue and ecru strips alternate. Study the block assembly diagram (Figure E). Complete fifteen B blocks.

Figure D

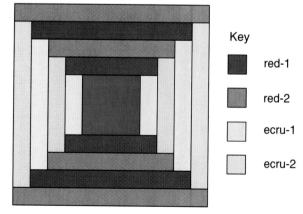

Key

red-1	
red-2	
ecru-1	
ecru-2	

Block A

Figure E

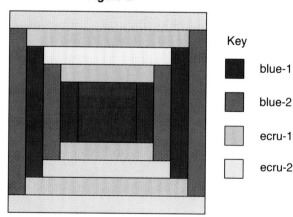

Key

blue-1	
blue-2	
ecru-1	
ecru-2	

Block B

Finishing the Quilt

1. Follow the instructions in the Virginia Reel Quilt to trim the blocks to 16½ inches square and trim a ⅜-inch square of batting only out of each corner (Figure F).

Figure F

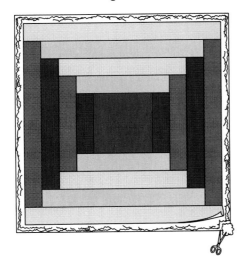

Figure G

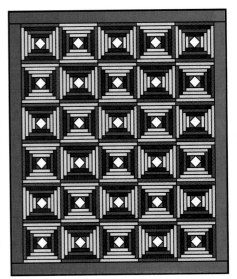

2. Assemble the blocks into six horizontal rows of five blocks each. Study the completed quilt layout (Figure G) very carefully, paying special attention to the orientation of the colors in the blocks.

3. Join the blocks with finishing strips, just as for the Virginia Reel Quilt (page 60). Cut twenty-four strips on the lengthwise grain, 1½ inches wide by 18 inches long.

4. The horizontal rows are joined together with finishing strips in the same manner. Cut strips 1½ inches wide by approximately 2 inches longer than the length of the rows to be joined. (The completed quilt interior should measure 80½ by 96½ inches, including ¼-inch seam allowances.) Press the quilt top.

5. Add a 5-inch border for this quilt by the standard Quilt-As-You-Sew method. (Refer to pages 193–195 for details.)

6. Use a ⅝-inch French-fold binding to complete the quilt. (Refer to page 198.)

Variation

For a queen/double quilt with fewer blocks, make twenty blocks; assemble, add borders, and finish according to the directions for the Virginia Reel Quilt (pages 59–62).

FEED DOGS UP: UNMARKED SURFACE DESIGNS

The beauty of unmarked, or pattern-free, quilting is that you are the only person who knows if it came out the way you intended. In contrast, it is usually quite easy to spot deviations in straight lines, grids, or cables that were marked before stitching. Pattern-free quilting eliminates the search for a perfect quilting design in just the right size and shape. It cuts out the time-consuming, laborious task of marking the quilt top. It prevents apprehension about whether the marks can be removed.

QUILTING FOR PEOPLE WHO CAN'T SEW A STRAIGHT LINE

It is hard to ruin the random curved lines in the next group of projects. For most people the hardest part is the uncertainty of "getting it right," and that is easily overcome with a little practice. Our sample project is a pillow and a variation, but the idea is easily adapted to other projects, such as a vest with wavy vertical lines and an echo-quilted collar (Diagram 1). Or suppose you are quilting a Triple Irish Chain "in the ditch" and you get to the blank alternate block (Diagram 2). Instead of worrying about marking and keeping straight lines, just let them wave! It isn't necessary to repeat the lines three times. The wavy gridwork provides enough design.

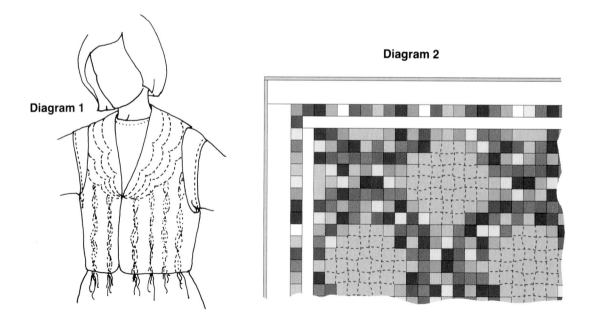

Diagram 1

Diagram 2

SIZE

12½ inches square

MATERIALS REQUIRED

⅜ yard of Ultrasuede™ for front and back

⅛ yard of Ultrasuede for binding

Scraps for heart appliqués

12½-inch square of batting

12½-inch square of muslin to back quilting

Polyester filling

Basic Heart Pillow

Cutting the Fabric

1. Cut two 12½-inch squares from Ultrasuede for the pillow front and back. Cut one 12½-inch square from quilt batting and muslin.
2. Use the heart pattern to cut four hearts from scrap fabric for appliqué.
3. For the Ultrasuede binding, cut two strips 1½ inches wide by 12½ inches long and two strips 1½ inches wide by 13 inches long.

71

Figure A

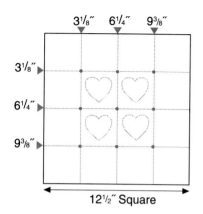

3⅛″   6¼″   9⅜″

3⅛″

6¼″

9⅜″

← 12½″ Square →

Heart
Pattern

Appliquéing the Hearts

1. Lightly mark the grid (Figure A), or just mark dots as indicated where those lines would cross.

2. In the four center squares, use your favorite method to appliqué the hearts in place. Leave part of one side open, stuff the hearts lightly with fiberfill and complete the appliqué. You may prefer to quilt first and appliqué after the lines are in place.

Quilting the Pillow

Layer the pillow front right sideup on top of the quilt batting. Quilt between the appliqués (see Figures B-1–B-3 below) or as desired.

You may want to practice making the meandering lines with a pencil and paper first. The plan, of course, is to look like there is no plan and that you naturally create wonderful lines.

Mark a guideline that is straight. Use an easily removed visible mark or make a crease line by running a needle point along the edge of an acrylic ruler. The crease line will not be visible for long; mark it right before stitching.

In this case, three lines were stitched along each line of the grid. The first line gently meanders back and forth across the marked straight line. It is a good idea to establish the maximum distance you will curve away from the line in either direction. On these pillows that is about 5/16 inch.

As the second line meanders generally opposite the first, be careful not to cross the marked line at the same points. Crossing at different locations prevents creating a mirror image (Figure B-1). With the third line, make a path between the first two in some way. If it doesn't look random enough, you can always add another line to distract from too much regularity. Complete as shown in Figures B-2 and B-3.

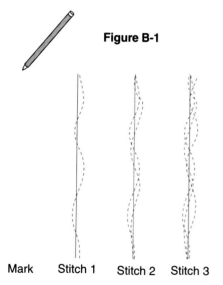

Figure B-1

Mark   Stitch 1   Stitch 2   Stitch 3

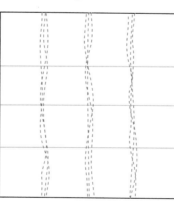

Figure B-2

All three vertical rows stitched and horizontal rows marked

Figure B-3

Assembling the Pillow

Instead of being made traditionally, the Ultrasuede pillow is assembled like a quilt, with wrong sides facing. The binding is added like quilt binding.

1. Fold the binding strips in half lengthwise, wrong sides facing. To eliminate raw edges on the longer binding strips, fold under the extra ¼ inch at each end, before folding the strips in half lengthwise.
2. Lay a 12½-inch strip along one side of the pillow top, with right sides facing and raw edges even. Stitch in place. Sew the other 12½-inch strip in place on the opposite side of the pillow, in the same manner. The remaining binding strips will be added later.
3. Layer the pillow top and bottom wrong sides facing. Fold the binding around the pillow edges and slip-stitch to the bottom of the pillow.
4. Add the remaining binding strips in the same manner as steps 2 and 3, including the previously sewn strips in the stitching. Be sure to leave one side of the pillow partially open to add stuffing.
5. Add stuffing. Slip-stitch the opening closed and carefully stitch the ends of the binding shut.

Homespun Heart Pillow

Select fabric for ruffles. The pillow shown (see page 71) has two ruffles, a purchased 1½-inch-wide ecru ruffle and a second ruffle 2½ inches wide. For the second ruffle you will need approximately ¾ yard of fabric.

Making and Adding a Single Ruffle

If you wish, you can make your own ruffles. It's easy.

1. Cut a fabric strip lengthwise, twice the desired finished width, plus two ½-inch seam allowances. Piece as necessary for the desired length, two to two and one-half times the perimeter of the pillow. Lightweight fabrics and wider ruffles look better with extra fullness. For the 2½-inch ruffle shown on the Homespun pillow, cut and piece fabric as necessary to obtain a strip 6 inches wide by 150 inches long.
2. Fold and press the fabric strip lengthwise with wrong sides facing. Machine-baste two rows of stitching approximately 3/16 inch apart, close to the raw edges. Gather the ruffle to the desired length by pulling up on the threads.
3. Starting at the center of one side, rather than at a corner, pin the ruffle to the pillow top, raw edges matching and the ruffle lying on the pillow top. Adjust the fullness around the pillow, allowing extra fullness at the corners.

   When the ruffle is pinned all around the pillow top, overlap the seam ends so that no raw edges will be visible from the front (Figure C).
4. Baste the ruffle to the pillow top, using a ½-inch seam allowance.

Figure C

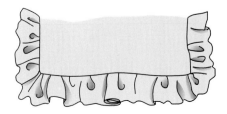

Assembling the Pillow

Whether you make your own or purchase the ruffles, here's what you do.

1. Layer the pillow top and the narrow ruffle right sides facing, raw edges even. Pin in position, overlapping the seam ends along one side. Layer the wide second ruffle on top of the first ruffle, overlapping the ends in the same place. Baste in position through all layers.
2. Place the pillow top and bottom right sides facing. Sew all around the outside edge, leaving an opening along one side for turning. Clip the corners of the seam allowance diagonally.
3. Turn the pillow right side out. Stuff tightly, pushing stuffing into the corners of the pillow. Slip-stitch the opening closed.

BEYOND ZIGZAG: DECORATIVE MACHINE QUILTING

Decorative machine quilting means using the decorative stitches built into the sewing machine for the actual quilting stitch. The most common decorative stitch is the zigzag. Some people even prefer a narrow zigzag over a straight stitch for in-the-ditch quilting. Zigzag is also commonly used on the outside edge of fused patchwork or appliqué designs, usually with invisible thread, to secure the fabric and quilt it at the same time. However, since we want to move beyond the basics you have probably already tried, let's start with buttonhole-stitch appliqué. This technique is very appropriate when you want a quilt to have a 1930s look. Use the buttonhole stitch on printed appliqué user-friendly fabric and no one will believe that you did not hand-appliqué the whole thing. The combination of fusing and machine quilting makes our next project, a charming scrap quilt, a snap to make. You'll get a chance to use all your machine's decorative stitches in the project after that.

Scrappy Star Wall Hanging

SIZE

26 inches square
Block Size: 4½ inches square

MATERIALS REQUIRED

Sixteen 4¼-inch square scraps of
assorted fabric for stars

Sixteen 4-inch squares of paper-backed
fusible web or film

Sixteen 5-inch square scraps of
assorted fabric for background

Assorted contrasting thread for
machine-quilting star blocks

⅛ yard of red fabric for border (cut
crosswise)

⅛ yard of brown fabric for border (cut
crosswise)

¾ yard of blue fabric for border and
binding

Approximately 29 inches square of
batting

Approximately 29 inches square of
backing fabric

Optional: nylon monofilament thread
for machine quilting

Nine ½- to ¾-inch buttons

Red thread for buttons and assorted
threads for buttonhole stitch

Selecting the Fabric

Think theme. In this case it was country, carried out with a basic antique color scheme of navy, turkey red, and camel. This quilt would also look great in many other combinations, such as red, white, and blue assorted star and stripe prints, or bold jewel-tone geometrics.

Don't overmatch. The fact that there are different camels, reds, and even greens makes the surface interesting.

Look for contrast. The quilt will be more pleasing if the fabrics cover a wide range of styles (floral, stripes, geometrics) and offer a density of design with light and dark, from busy to calm.

Select in pairs. Choose a star and its companion background fabric, then set the pair aside. Accumulate about sixteen pairs and look at the fabrics as a group for balance before cutting.

Appliquéing the Individual Stars

Fusible appliqué was the method of choice for this wall hanging. Fuse each star to a 5-inch square of background fabric.

Fusible Appliqué   Many varieties of paper-backed fusible materials are available, and instructions vary widely. Please read and follow carefully the manufacturer's instructions.

1. Rough-cut a piece of paper-backed fusible material larger than the pattern pieces to be cut.

SCRAPPY STAR APPLIQUÉ PATTERN

SCRAPPY STAR SQUARE PATTERN

2. Trace the pattern onto the paper backing. If the pattern piece is not symmetrical, place the pattern piece right side down on the paper before tracing. If the pattern piece is symmetrical, no special instructions are needed. Apply the fusible material to the wrong side of a piece of fabric that is slightly larger than the paper.

3. Cut the pattern but do not remove the paper backing from the pattern piece yet.

4. Mark the base fabric for the appliqué placement. After cutting all the pattern pieces, position them on the marked base fabric for accuracy.

5. Peel off the paper backing. Fuse the star into position on each square. I position the star and then just tap the piece with the tip of the iron. Check the positioning again before completing with a full iron press.

6. Finishing the edge of fused appliqué is not absolutely necessary, but it is recommended if the piece will be handled or laundered frequently. For a sewn finish, go over the edges with a narrow zigzag stitch.

Completing the Star Blocks

1. Finish the edges of the star with machine stitching. The stars shown are finished with a machine buttonhole stitch in a contrasting color. This was actually done with stitch 14 on a Pfaff 1473CD. However, many machines have a buttonhole stitch included in the decorative stitches. Other decorative stitches or a loose zigzag could be substituted. Make a test stitch to decide. Practice turning the corners with the selected stitch.

2. Complete 16 star blocks.

Assembling the Quilt Top

1. Arrange the sixteen star blocks into four rows of four blocks each so that they have a random scrap look. See the completed wall hanging layout (Figure A).

2. Sew the blocks together into rows.

3. Sew the rows together.

Adding the Borders

The borders for this quilt are ⅝ inch , 1 inch, and 2 inches finished, added the Good Old-fashioned Way. (Refer to pages 192–193.)

Layering and Quilting

1. Layer the quilt top with batting and backing as on page 182.

2. Machine-quilt with invisible monofilament thread in the ditch between all star blocks and before the red border.

3. Use the buttonhole stitch to machine-quilt between the red and brown and between the brown and blue borders. This stitching goes through all three layers.

Completing the Wall Hanging

1. A ⅜-inch French-fold binding finishes the wall hanging. (Refer to page 198.)

2. Nine assorted antique-looking buttons are sewn in the corners of the central blocks with red thread (see the photograph).

Figure A

Fence Rail Sampler

Early on I discovered that most of the decorative stitch illustrations in my sewing machine manuals do not begin to do the stitches justice. The only way to know how the stitches on your machine are going to look is to stitch them. This Fence Rail Sampler wall hanging, stitched on a Pfaff 1473 CD, gives you that opportunity. Just follow the instructions below and you'll have a personal sampler that shows off your machine's repertoire. A pocket sewn on the back keeps a list of the stitches used handy for future reference. If you enjoy this project, you're bound to like the decoratively stitched Picnic Basket Quilt (pages 144–151) and Iris Lee's Machine Crazy Quilting (page 176).

[Do you notice the clever kaleidoscope in the photograph? Available in kit form (see Resources, pages 202–203), it is easily assembled and can be used to show off assorted machine decorative stitches sewn in a sampling of threads.]

Selecting the Fabric

The photographed quilt features purple and raspberry fabrics and threads, but any two contrasting fabrics with matching decorative rayon threads may be chosen. When stitching, the threads will be used on the contrasting, not the matching, fabrics.

Cutting the Fabric

1. Cut 6-inch squares of fabric, six from purple and six from raspberry. The finished block size is 4 inches, so the blocks will be trimmed to 4½ inches after the decorative stitching is completed, but before the blocks are joined. The blocks are cut slightly oversize for ease during stitching.
2. Also cut twenty-four 6-inch squares of medium-weight nonwoven interfacing. Each quilt block will be backed with two layers of interfacing to stabilize the stitching.

Marking and Stitching the Blocks

1. Use a water-erasable marking pen to mark a vertical center line on each block, lengthwise along the grain. Mark two more lines on each side of the center line, spacing the lines ¾ inch apart (Figure A).
2. Layer each block right side up on top of two layers of interfacing, using pins to hold in position until the first line of stitching is completed.
3. Use contrasting rayon thread and the decorative stitch of your choice to stitch along the center line of the quilt block, centering the stitching over the marked line. Using a denser stitch for the center row gives the block a more balanced appearance.
4. Continue stitching along the rows, alternating sides of the block as you go. Be certain that the fabric and interfacing are smooth before stitching, to avoid puckers.
5. Complete all twelve blocks in the same manner.

Assembling the Quilt Top

1. Before assembling the blocks, trim each block to 4½ inches square, which includes ¼-inch seam allowances. This is most easily done with a large square acrylic ruler and the rotary cutter.

Trim the interfacing away close to the last row of stitching along the loose edges of each block. These are the edges that run in the same

SIZE
20 × 24 inches
Block Size: 4 inches square

MATERIALS REQUIRED
½ yard of purple fabric for blocks and border
½ yard of raspberry fabric for blocks and border
¾ yard of medium-weight nonwoven interfacing
¾ yard of purple print fabric for border and French-fold binding
⅝ yard of fabric for backing
⅝ yard of lightweight cotton batting
Water-erasable marking pen

Figure A

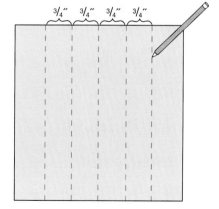

direction as the stitching. When the blocks are assembled in the alternating fashion, only two layers of interfacing will be sewn into the seam allowance of each pair.

2. Arrange the blocks into four rows of three blocks each, alternating the block colors as well as the direction of stitching (Figure B).

3. Sew the blocks into rows. Sew the rows together. The quilt interior should measure 12½ by 16½ inches, including ¼-inch seam allowances.

Figure B

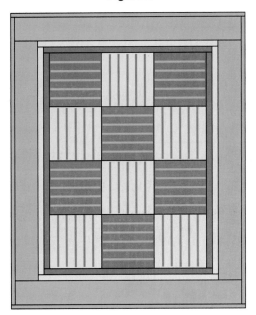

Layering the Quilt Top and Adding the Borders

Because this quilt features borders added by the Modified Quilt-As-You-Sew method, the quilt is layered with batting and backing first. (Refer to page 196.) The borders for this quilt are ½ inch, ½ inch, and 2½ inches finished.

Quilting

Stitch in the ditch between all quilt blocks using invisible thread.

Finishing the Quilt

A ⅜-inch French-fold binding completes the quilt. (Refer to page 198 for details.)

Coming Soon

As sewing machines enter the computer age, new models are becoming available that will allow us to program our own decorative stitches. That means I can create new designs or adapt a favorite quilting motif to programmable stitches. This capability didn't mean as much when 9 mm (less than ½ inch) was the maximum width of the stitch, but now many machines can be programmed to stitch 40 mm wide, or close to 1⅝ inches, and upcoming models are bound to go wider. By taking advantage of the mirror-image stitching feature, I can make up a design that will very nicely fill a 3½- or 4-inch border or sashing strip. With the "start stitch at beginning" feature, I can always be sure mirror-imaged or multiple rows start from the same position. Programmable decorative stitches like these are sure to show up on quilts soon (Figure C). They will let quilters stitch perfect symmetric patterns without marking.

Figure C

QUILTING IN THE DITCH

Quilting in the ditch with invisible thread or machine-tying a quilt are two easy ways to quilt a crib-sized piece when layering a quilt traditionally. On full-sized bed quilts, quilting in the ditch is not so easy because the extra weight of the quilt is harder to manage. Some people like to work their way up to a task requiring more skill, while others plunge in and take a sink-or-swim approach. This book is written in the "work-your-way-up" style. If you want to plunge in, read the crib quilt instructions; then make a full-sized quilt top and go on to Chapter 10 to learn how to quilt it.

The quilt block called Log Cabin is composed of numerous strips of fabric that spiral around a center square. Typically, the strips on two adjacent sides of the center square are dark, and on the two remaining sides they are light. This creates a strong diagonal visual line in the block. The nine-patch blocks in this Mock Log Cabin Quilt use squares and triangles to create the same diagonal design effect with fewer pieces and quicker assembly (Figures A-1, A-2).

Figure A-2

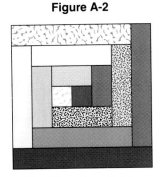

Figure A-1

Mock Log Cabin
Quilt Block

Traditional Log Cabin
Quilt Block

The same pink print fabric is repeated for the center square in each Mock Log Cabin block and creates a subtle secondary pattern. As in the traditional Log Cabin, the block is divided diagonally into light and dark halves. For this crib quilt, assorted pinks and blues were used as darks, and assorted ecrus were selected as lights. Using the same ecru fabric for all the light pieces is an option that would make fabric selection easier.

The Log Cabin block is so popular and used in so many different arrangements that even the way the blocks are set or arranged has a name. This particular arrangement of blocks in concentric diamonds is called "Barn Raising."

Cutting the Fabric

To complete the forty-eight blocks needed for the quilt, you can cut each piece individually; but this quilt is well suited to scrap strip piecing to make the squares and Sew-Before-You-Cut triangles. Instructions are included for both methods. It is ironic that the instructions for quick techniques are much longer to write than those for traditional piecing, but if you have not used these techniques, please try them this time.

Cutting Squares and Triangles Traditionally Using Pattern A, cut 144 squares from light fabrics, 144 squares from dark fabrics, and 48 squares from the fabric chosen for the center square. Using Pattern B, cut ninety-six assorted dark triangles and ninety-six assorted light triangles. Proceed to make the blocks, joining a dark triangle to each light triangle (Figure B).

Cutting and Sewing the Squares with Strip Techniques To cut and sew the squares do the following:

1. Cut seven strips 2½ inches wide by 18 inches long from the fabric selected for the center square. The rotary cutter makes it quick work.

2. Use a rotary cutter and acrylic ruler to measure and cut the fabric. Cut assorted light and dark fabric strips 2½ inches wide, of varying lengths up to 14 inches long. The minimum total length needed for both dark strips and light strips is approximately 360 inches, or enough to cut 144

SIZE

43 × 55 inches
Block Size: 6 inches square

MATERIALS REQUIRED

1⅜ yards of assorted pink and blue fabrics for blocks
½ yard of pink fabric for center square of each block
1⅜ yards of assorted ecru fabrics for blocks
¼ yard of pink print fabric for border, cut crosswise and pieced
¾ yard of blue floral fabric for border
1¾ yards of backing fabric, 60 inches wide
1¾ yards of batting, or crib-size packaged batting
⅝ yard for French-fold binding
8 yards of ribbon or 16 yards of yarn for tying

Figure C

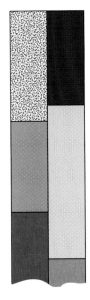

Figure B

MOCK LOG CABIN

Pattern Piece
A

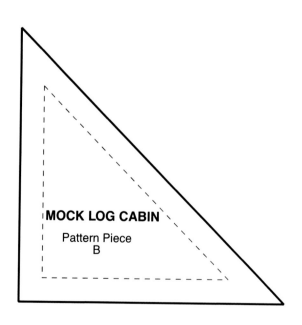

MOCK LOG CABIN

Pattern Piece
B

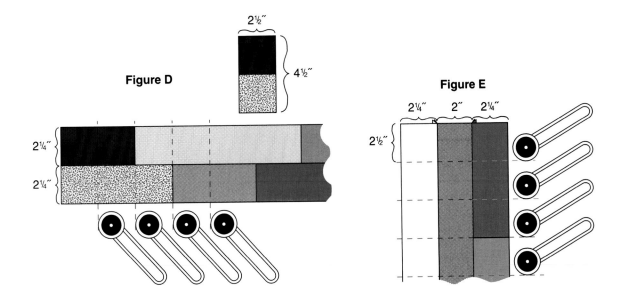

Figure D

2½"

4½"

2¼"

2¼"

Figure E

2¼" 2" 2¼"

2½"

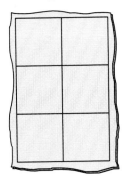

Figure F

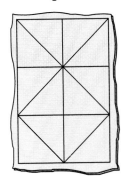

Figure G

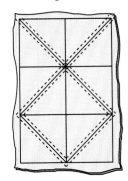

Figure H

segments 2½ inches square. Sew random-length dark pieces together, end to end, using a ¼-inch seam allowance. Make long strips. Sew two strips together, side by side (Figure C). Duplicate with light pieces.

3. Cut across the two-strip sets every 2½ inches (Figure D). These segments will be used as "pairs of squares" when assembling the unit block. A total of forty-eight pairs of squares (segments) from assorted dark scraps is needed. There will be some waste when the seams are in the middle of the next square. Just cut away the seam and continue cutting.

4. In the same manner, make forty-eight pairs of squares from assorted light scraps.

5. Assemble single strips of dark fabrics on one side of the center square fabric strips. Then add light strips to the other side of the center square fabric strips. Press the seam allowances away from the center.

6. From these assembled strip sets cut forty-eight strip segments 2½ inches square (Figure E).

Making Sew-Before-You-Cut Triangles A "pieced square" is a pair of triangles sewn together to make a square (Figure B). Ninety-six light/dark pieced squares are needed for the blocks in this quilt. To avoid having the same fabrics repeated in all the pieced squares, make nine sets of twelve, pairing different fabrics in each set. There will be a few extra.

1. Cut fabric pieces approximately 6½ by 10 inches from nine dark and nine light fabrics.

2. Pair fabrics right sides facing, making sets of dark/light. Secure.

3. On the wrong side of the lighter fabric in each pair, use a ruler and marker to mark a grid of six 2⅞-inch squares (Figure F).

4. The cutting lines are marked before the fabric is stitched. Draw diagonal lines through the squares (Figure G). Draw the lines in the same direction as the illustration and you will be able to sew continuously.

5. Stitch through both layers of fabric on both sides of the drawn lines, using accurate ¼-inch seam allowances (Figure H).

6. Cut triangles apart on every drawn line, and open them to get twelve pieced squares from each drawn grid of six squares.

Making the Block

Assemble forty-eight blocks (Figure I). If you have cut traditionally, lay pieces out to match the diagram and assemble into rows first, then blocks.

If you have used the quick-piecing techniques, each block is already partially assembled. Use one dark pair of squares, one light pair of squares, and two light/dark pieced squares to complete the top and bottom rows. Add them to the center strip set of squares to complete the block

Each completed block should measure 6½ inches square, including ¼-inch seam allowances.

Assembling the Quilt Top

1. Lay out the blocks in eight rows of six blocks each, carefully checking the orientation of the design. See the completed crib quilt layout (Figure J). Study the block assembly and rearrange if necessary to avoid a concentration of a particular fabric in one area, but don't go crazy rearranging blocks.
2. Join the blocks in each row, and join the rows together. The completed quilt top should measure 36½ by 48½ inches, including ¼-inch seam allowances.

Figure I

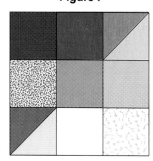

Figure J

86

Adding the Borders

The photographed quilt features a 1⅛-inch pink print border and a 2-inch blue floral border, added the Good Old-fashioned Way (pages 192–193).

Layering a Crib Quilt

The basic information for layering a crib quilt and that for layering a full-sized bed quilt are the same. However, as the quilts get larger, more variations, questions, and difficulties may arise. (See Chapter 10, "Whole-Quilt Machine Quilting," for more detailed information.)

1. The backing fabric should be around 2 inches bigger in all directions than the size of the finished quilt. With this quilt that is very close to the standard 45-inch-wide fabric. You should not have to piece the backing, but it may not have much extra allowance. Press carefully.

   Cut the batting the same size, steaming if necessary to remove wrinkles and bumps. (See the discussion of preparing batting on pages 180–181.)

2. Use a table for the layering process. Center the backing wrong side up on the table. I hear people talk about taping and clamping the backing fabric and making sure it is very taut. I don't do that and have never had a problem I felt could have been solved by a taut backing.

   Layer the batting next, centered and carefully smoothed. Finally, center and layer the pressed quilt top, right side up.

3. Pin baste or thread baste. I prefer the small safety pins, because using them does not require lifting the quilt sandwich, which can distort the arrangement. Start in the center and work out, pinning or sewing through all layers. The minimum number of pins on this quilt is one in the center of each block, or forty-eight pins. It is better to start with more pins than you think you need and eliminate as you become more experienced.

Quilting a Crib Quilt

For most of the in-the-ditch quilting, I like to use the smoky invisible monofilament nylon thread for the top thread only. In the bobbin use a 100% cotton or cotton-wrapped polyester thread that matches the color of the backing fabric. (See page 32 for a discussion of thread.)

It is usually necessary to loosen the tension when using the nylon thread (page 32). It is very stretchy and if the tension is too tight, the thread stretches while sewn and draws up, then puckers when you stop sewing. Use a stitch length of 8 to 10 stitches per inch for quilting.

To keep the quilt manageable when machine quilting, it is necessary to roll and fold it into a smaller package. This way you control the quilt. Just as when training a dog, you must make sure the quilt knows who is in charge.

1. The longest, usually the vertical, center seam is the first seam that will be sewn. Roll the right edge of the quilt up to within 4 or 5 inches of the center seam (Figure K). Fold the left side of the quilt in 5- or 6-inch folds until it is 4 or 5 inches from the center seam (Figure L).

2. To complete the package, roll your quilt, like a sleeping bag (Figure M).

3. Move to the machine; position the end of the first seam you are quilting under the needle. Hold the remainder of the quilt in your lap.

Figure K

Figure L

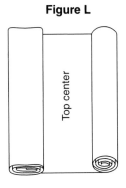

Figure M

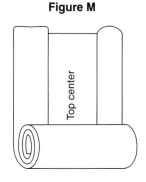

4. As you begin to quilt, use both hands to pull away from the seam, making the ditch to stitch in. Gradually unroll the "sleeping bag" end of the quilt as you sew to prevent any pressure on the needle. When you are working on a small piece, such as this quilt, the addition of extra tables and work surface is not necessary.

5. When you have finished the first seam, reroll the quilt and prepare to quilt the center horizontal seam. After that I usually continue to work out from the center of the quilt, sewing one or two horizontal seams on each side of the center, then switching back to vertical, and so on.

To maintain control of the quilt, it must be rerolled at least every couple of seams and sometimes every seam. As you reroll, check the quilt back for newly sewn pleats. Little puckers are often found at seam crossings, and my personal decision is not to take them out. Large tucks, however, must be corrected. But you make your personal decision about your quilt. (These little tucks are more likely to happen with polyester batting than with cotton. The polyester is slick, and the fabric can slide. With cotton batting the quilt fabric and batting almost stick to each other.)

Finishing the Quilt

A ⅜-inch pink French-fold binding finishes the quilt. (See page 198 for details.) Each center square is machine-tied. Read on for ideas.

MACHINE TYING

Tying fulfills the requirement that all three layers of the quilt be attached. Machine tying just hurries the process along. And you can achieve some very nice effects with contrasting thread. Not only is this Mock Log Cabin machine quilted, but each block is "tied" in the pink center square. You could choose to tie more frequently and eliminate quilting entirely. There are several tying methods:

1. Use a machine zigzag stitch, with both the stitch width and length set close to zero. Hold threads behind the needle, and stitch several times through all layers. This will secure the threads. Adjust the stitch width to about ¼ inch wide and stitch eight to ten times; then adjust back to zero and stitch a few times more to secure the threads. Trim the loose ends.

2. If you have decorative stitches available on your machine, experiment with a decorative stitch instead of zigzag. This is particularly easy if you have the ability to instruct your machine to stitch one complete design and then stop. It is especially fun with some of the cute designs available.

3. For the finishing method used on this quilt, cut a 3- to 6-inch length of ribbon for each center square. Tie the ribbon into a bow, center it on the square, and secure it to the quilt with a narrow zigzag stitch across the bow.

4. Or finally, you might want to simulate a quilt hand-tied with yarn. Cut 9- to 12-inch lengths of yarn. Secure the center point of each yarn piece in the center of the appropriate squares using the same stitching pattern as method 1. After the yarn is secured, tie in a square knot and trim the ends as desired.

CONTINUOUS-CURVE AND OUTLINE QUILTING

Our next topic is a first look at how hand-quilted surface patterns might appear when done by machine. Outline quilting is a common hand-quilting technique. As the name implies, the stitching follows the shape, or outline, of the patchwork pieces, usually ¼ inch from the seam but sometimes a little less (Diagram 3). The finished look is neat, crisp, and traditional, and the stitching requires little creativity and no marking.

When done by machine with the feed dogs up, outline quilting has three drawbacks. First, it involves a lot of stopping and turning—easy with a small piece like a pillow top but next to impossible with a large quilt. Second, the continual stopping and starting leaves many loose thread ends to deal with. And finally, it is challenging to sew a straight line parallel to the adjacent seam. Because of these problems and other people's lukewarm attitude toward machine-guided outline quilting, I never actually tried it on anything larger than a pillow square—until I was writing this book.

The Continuous-Curve Breakthrough

The three drawbacks to outline quilting mentioned earlier must be what caused Barbara Johannah to think of the method she calls continuous-curve quilting. With her method the stitching line curves in a gentle arc from one end of a patchwork seam to the other, crossing gracefully at the corners. Generally, the widest part of the arc is about ¼ inch from the seam line (Diagram 4-A). This method reduces much of the stop-and-start aspect of machine outline quilting yet produces a finished effect similar to that of outline quilting.

Remember, the continuous-curve quilting being discussed here is with the feed dogs up. The discussion won't really be complete until you read the section on free-motion continuous-curve quilting (pages 108–109), which is done with the feed dogs down. The real benefit there is the elimination of even more turning. (Combining Barbara's method with free-motion quilting and then promoting the new technique is generally credited to Harriet Hargrave.)

If you look ahead to a project called Teacup Pillow Sham (pages 102–104), you will see the similarity between it and Barbara's continuous-curve quilting. To me, continuous curve is quite attractive as a secondary pattern on patchwork that is predominantly squares. I am not as enthusiastic about it on triangles, diamonds, and other shapes. I've also discovered that I prefer not to attempt either machine-guided or free-motion continuous curves larger than 2½ inches. It is too hard for me to control the gradual change that creates the arc, and I think that arcs are not worth marking. You, however, should try as many different techniques as interest you. Your goal is to find methods you like, not to adapt to what I like.

Diagram 3

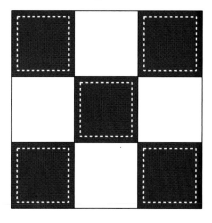

Diagram 4-A

Continuous Curve Quilting,
Every Square

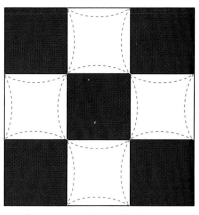

Continuous Curve Quilting,
Every Other Square

Diagram 4-B

Modified Outline Quilting,
Every Square

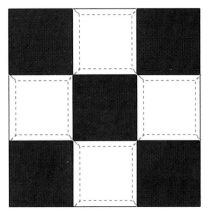

Modified Outline Quilting,
Every Other Square

Modified Outline Quilting

Modified outline quilting (Diagram 4-B) is a variation on the continuous-curve approach. In modified outline quilting, x's are created at each intersection, with straight stitching in between. To me, it captures some of the crispness of hand outline quilting. I also find it easier to stitch a consistent distance from the seam than to establish consistent curves. The bad part is that there is a definite turn that requires lifting the presser foot, a step that is not necessary with continuous curve and that would be very demanding on small individual pieces. Although it takes longer, I like the look better.

Developing Stitching Sequences

To be more efficient at continuous-curve and outline quilting, you need to develop a stitching sequence that eliminates as many stops, starts, and loose thread ends as possible. With machine-guided feed-dogs-up methods, this means moving from one edge of the quilt to the other in as smooth and direct a path as possible (Diagram 5). You need to keep only a small amount of the quilt "loose" or flexible enough to turn, since it is not necessary to turn the entire quilt very often.

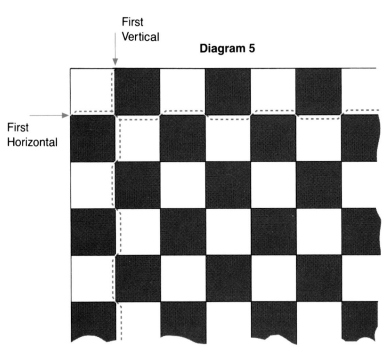

First
Vertical

Diagram 5

First
Horizontal

Figuring out the best sequence is really a paper-and-pencil puzzle. The need for a clear path is more crucial in machine-guided (feed-dogs-up) quilting because the quilt can be turned in small increments only. To develop a sequence, make a photocopy of the quilt top block layout and lay a sheet of tracing paper over it. Then, without lifting your pencil, draw a line through the patchwork design from one edge to another, keeping as direct a path as possible. Repeat until you have worked out the stitching sequence for the entire quilt. (By the way, unless the individual pieces are larger than 2 inches square, quilting in either the foreground or the background of a block design is usually enough.)

If a quilt has an easy stitch sequence, machine-guided outline quilting is much easier than it sounds, and the look is very neat. The feed-dogs-up position ensures that the stitches are smooth, straight, and uniform. In fact, even stitching is the main reason you will choose it. You will discover that no matter how good you are at free-motion quilting, you will never be able to keep the stitches at a consistent length the way your sewing machine feed dogs can.

To understand how I came to many of these conclusions, let me tell you about my Flying Geese Quilt. I made the quilt a couple of years ago, intending it to be a combination hand- and machine-quilting project. The pieced interior (minus the borders) was layered on full-sized batting and backing. The long strips between the geese were machine-quilted in the ditch. The borders were added using the Modified Quilt-As-You-Sew method, and the outside border was machine-quilted in a free-form, free-motion style. The only part remaining was the geese, which I planned to outline-quilt by hand. I had about five geese quilted in each row, and then the project got stalled. Rather than give up, I got the idea of quilting randomly on the remaining geese. That way, I rationalized, I could use the quilt and pretend that no more quilting was intended. Yet any time it was convenient to quilt a little, I could stitch around a few triangles, until one day, all the geese would be quilted. (You can tell my mind had moved from rationalizing to fantasizing!) Instead, as you can imagine, all progress on hand quilting ceased after about fifteen geese were randomly quilted.

As I was writing this book, the Flying Geese Quilt came to mind as a way to demonstrate the beauty of continuous-curve quilting. Well, I was wrong. The first thing I discovered was that making a gradual continuous curve on a piece as large as these triangles was difficult. The second thing I learned, to my surprise, was that outline quilting on a full-sized quilt can actually be easy. I found the Flying Geese strips allowed me to keep stitching in one basic direction (Diagram 6). Even though the stitching goes straight in from the stripe and diagonally out toward the stripe, it still moves from the top to the bottom of the quilt.

Diagram 6

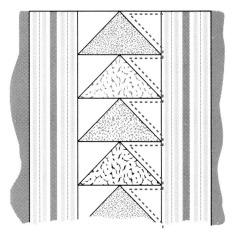

Flying Geese Quilt

The Flying Geese subunit is made with a large right-angle triangle in the center and two smaller right-angle triangles in the corners (Figure A). These subunits are pieced together in rows. The rows are joined by strips of fabric to make the quilt (Figure B).

Figure A

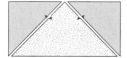

Figure B

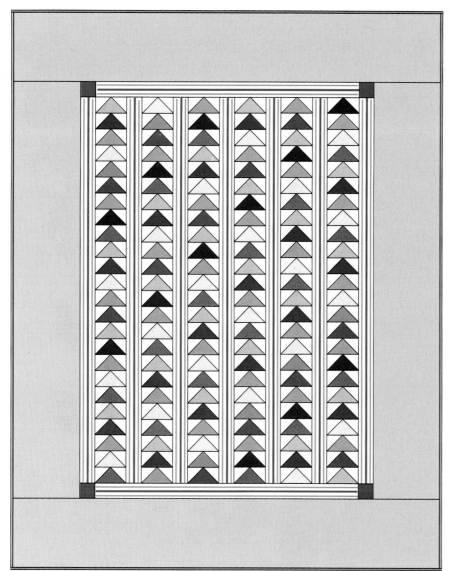

SIZE

80 × 99 inches
Subunit Size: 3 × 6 inches

MATERIALS REQUIRED

3½ yards of assorted pink, blue, and ecru fabrics for triangles

2¼ yards of striped fabric for strips and first border (preferred cuttable stripe repeat width is 4 inches)

2¾ yards of blue print fabric for border

5¾ yards of fabric for backing

5¾ yards of batting, or full-sized packaged batting

⅝ yard of fabric for French-fold binding

Water-erasable marking pen

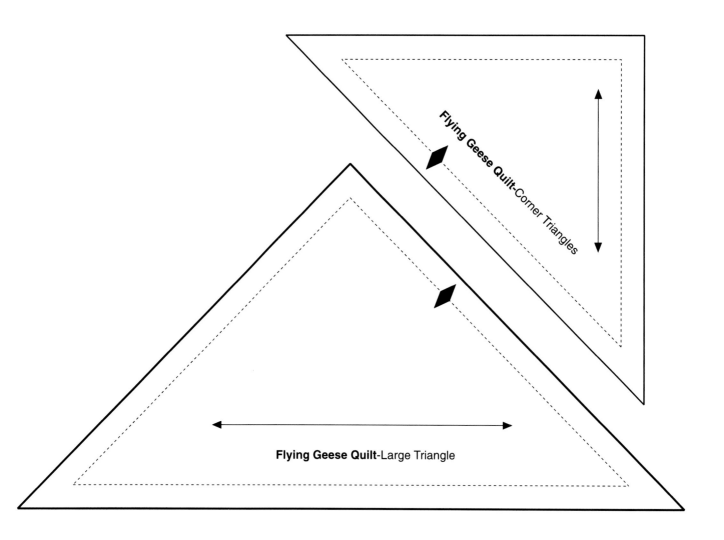

Flying Geese Quilt-Corner Triangles

Flying Geese Quilt-Large Triangle

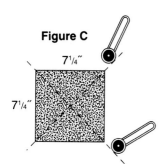

Figure C

7¼″

7¼″

Fabric Selection

The Flying Geese design is a favorite scrap quilt pieced completely from prints, with printed stripes used for the dividing strips. Select a striped fabric first, and then a minimum of fifteen to twenty different coordinating print fabrics for the large triangles, and at least seven or eight fabrics for the corners. Don't concentrate too hard on matching; the charm of a scrap quilt is its scrappy look. Pair each large triangle fabric with several different corner fabrics when assembling the subunits.

Cutting the Fabric

Use the pattern pieces provided to cut 144 large triangles (geese) and 288 small triangles (sky) from assorted prints, or rotary-cut as follows.

1. Cut thirty-six 7¼-inch squares from assorted prints. Cut each square twice diagonally (Figure C).

2. Cut 144 squares of 3⅞ inches from assorted prints. Cut each square once diagonally (Figure D).

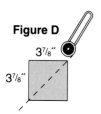

Figure D

3⅞″

3⅞″

Cutting the triangles as shown will result in sewing two bias edges together. However, this will allow all outside edges of the pieced subunit to be on the straight grain, which will ultimately result in a more stable quilt.

Chain Piecing the Subunits and Making Rows

1. Place one corner triangle on one large triangle, right sides facing. Align the hypotenuse of the corner triangle with the leg of the large triangle.
2. Sew these two triangles together. Be very careful not to stretch these two bias edges. Do not break the thread; continue sewing (Figure E). Link ten or twelve sets together.
3. Cut triangle sets apart and press seam allowances toward the large triangles.
4. Repeat, sewing a matching corner triangle to the opposite side of each large triangle.
5. Arrange as desired and sew the subunits together into six rows of twenty-four Flying Geese each. Be careful that the seam crosses just at the tip of each large triangle. Finished geese should be 3 inches tall. (This is very important.) Each completed row should measure 6½ inches wide by 72½ inches long, including ¼-inch seam allowances. Press the rows, pressing seam allowances at the bottom of each subunit down.

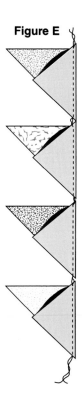

Figure E

Joining the Rows with Strips

Measure and compare the length of the vertical rows carefully. If necessary, adjust to make them equal. Look for subunits that are unusually large or small to make the adjustments.

1. Cut five joining strips. The mathematically correct cut size of the strips is 4 inches wide by 72½ inches long. If the stripe you have chosen is not this wide, you may make adjustments in the width of the strips or the borders to get the size quilt desired. Measure your pieced rows to determine how long to cut your strips.
2. Mark placement lines along both outside edges of each long fabric strip. Begin 3¼ inches from one end of a strip and mark every 3 inches (Figure F). Accuracy is essential for matching horizontal seam lines of the rows of Flying Geese from strip to strip.
3. With right sides facing and raw edges even, match the horizontal seam lines of the first rows of Flying Geese to the markings on the strip (Figure G). Sew together. Continue to complete the quilt interior. It should measure 54 by 72½ inches, including ¼-inch seam allowances. Press the seam allowances toward the striped strips.

Figure F

3¼"

3"

3"

3"

Adding the Borders, Quilting, and Binding

The first border finishes 3½ inches wide and has corner blocks. The final border finishes to 9½ inches wide. Both borders could be added using the Good Old-fashioned Way (pages 192–193) or the Modified Quilt-As-You-Sew Method (page 196), as you prefer. If the borders are not added Modified Quilt-As-You-Sew, quilt them in the ditch. The last border is free-motion quilted in a meandering style, feed dogs down. The quilt is finished with a ⅜-inch French-fold binding (refer to page 198).

Figure G

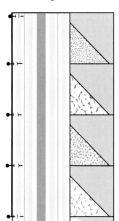

6

FEED DOGS UP: MARKED DESIGNS

If you have been reading this book from the beginning and paying close attention, you will have observed that at least two projects have had very simple markings—so simple, in fact, that the projects probably could have been completed without them. It is now time to get serious about quilting marked designs. As I promised in Chapter 3, we will be discussing marking tools, light tables, and stencils.

MARKING BASICS

In many ways, marking is more important for machine quilting than for hand quilting. With hand quilting you can stop and consider your options for the next stitch. With machine quilting you are moving quickly and need to know where you are going. Frequent stopping and starting interrupts your rhythm.

Remember that it is much easier to mark a quilt before it is layered. The marking, therefore, must withstand handling and still be visible during the actual quilting.

To mark quilts well requires both design skill and technical accuracy. In fact, around the turn of the last century, you could hire professional quilt markers to mark your quilt tops for you.

Fabric Selection

To me the first rule for quilting marked designs is to select fabrics that will enhance rather than hide the quilting. Even with machine quilting, the time it takes to find an appropriate quilting motif, mark it, quilt it, and then remove it is substantial. It is always sad to me when, after all that work, the quilting doesn't even show.

To show off quilting to advantage, use solid-color fabrics, very minimally printed designs, or contrasting thread. In fact, a large area of solid color looks very empty even lightly quilted and almost demands to be richly quilted, so go for it! In my own quilt making, I love working with prints and rarely use solids. Therefore, I have to decide consciously during the design stage where I want fancy quilting and must choose a solid or plain fabric that will show it off. Every time I stand back to look at the quilt in progress, I have to remind myself why that certain section looks so empty.

Marking Tools

If one marking method were perfect for every person and every quilt, there would only be one tool. This, however, is not the case.

Using a Light Table

If you do a lot of marking and don't already own a light table, it may be time to invest in one. The light illuminates the work surface from underneath, allowing you to trace a printed design directly onto fabric without using a stencil. It works as long as the fabric is not too dark. This table-top model is easy to store and reasonably priced. (See Resources, pages 202–203.)

By the bye, do you remember the sewing machine leaf for an extension table (page 28)? You can create a light table the same way with a translucent acrylic panel and a light source under the table. It looks strange when unexpected company arrives, but it works.

There are many different tools, each with advantages and disadvantages, and new ones are frequently offered. My advice is to try anything that looks good to you. Each of us has different eyesight, lighting level at the sewing machine, and preferences. In spite of the dozens of marking tools available, I have never gotten obsessed with trying them all. Generally, I rely on a few old standbys: water-erasable marking pens on light or medium colors and a white chalk wheel or silver pencil on dark fabrics.

Removing Marks

No matter which marking tool you choose, always test it on the fabric being used to make sure its mark is removable. Even chalk, which brushes off, should be tested to make sure it comes off easily.

Some people worry about the long-term effect of water-erasable pens on natural fibers. I've heard the same horror stories you have, but I still feel their ease and convenience outweigh the risk. I have been using water-erasable pens for fifteen years now with no disaster. I do advise that you follow the pen manufacturer's instructions, don't leave marks on any longer than necessary, and remove marks thoroughly. Never allow a marked quilt to come into contact with heat from an iron, a clothes dryer, or sunlight streaming through a window; even gentle heat has been known to set marks. If you are really concerned, completely submerge the finished quilt in cold water, without soap or any other additive that might react with the marking. This soaking should completely remove the marks and prevent color that could reappear later from hiding in the batting.

If a Mark Stays In

Every quilter I know panics if a mark is not easily removed. Yet as a collector of antique quilts, I see people reverently admiring antique quilts with visible pencil marks who say, "Oh look, it has never been washed!" So who knows? If the marking doesn't come out of your quilt, maybe a collector in the next century will consider it special.

Mock Marking

If you want to avoid marking but still want to quilt with a definite pattern, try some of these suggestions I call "mock marking."

One shortcut is to choose a fabric with a quiltable pattern and use it as the backing. Quilt on the "wrong" side and the bobbin thread shows up on the right side of the quilt. You must adjust the bobbin tension so that the stitch is perfectly balanced. You can adapt the same idea for borders, using print fabrics both as backing and as pattern design.

Another "quickie" is to purchase special paper preprinted with quilting designs. You just pin the paper in place, stitch along the design lines, and then tear the used paper away. Test to make sure your combination of paper, thread, and stitch size tears away relatively clean. It is a bore to pull out little pieces of paper with tweezers. I've made my own version using dress pattern tissue. I still have to mark the design, but I save the step of removing the markings.

CHANNELS AND GRIDS

Another way to get by with minimal marking is to use your sewing machine's quilting bar. This handy accessory lets you quilt allover straight-line patterns—channels, squares, diamonds, and 45- and 60-degree hanging diamonds—by marking just a few lines (Diagram 1).

Most machines come with a quilting bar accessory (Diagram 2). To use it you mark and stitch the first two parallel lines of the pattern, establishing the distance between them. For diamonds you must also stitch an intersecting line to establish the angle. Once those first few starter rows are stitched, no additional marking is needed. The quilting bar is set for the appropriate width, and as you sew, it "rides" along the adjacent stitching, guiding the new stitching in a straight, even path. It is a good idea to check the quilting bar occasionally if you are sewing a large piece. Sometimes the connection is a little loose, and in the process of moving a quilt, you can jar it out of position.

Diagram 2

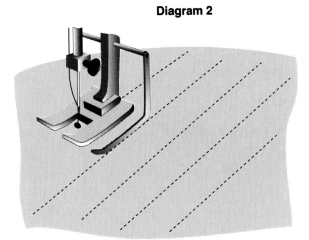

Diagram 1

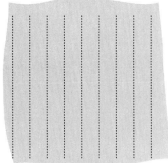

Channels

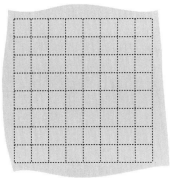

Squares

Diamonds

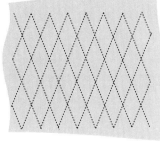

45° Diamonds

60° Diamonds

Machine-guided channel quilting (right) and diamond quilting (lower right) are made more interesting by using a double needle. The double row of stitching helps the quilting pop out more on this printed fabric.

Machine-guided all-over patterns are fun and fast to quilt. They can make plain fabric fancy for use in pillows, vests, or teddy bears. You can use them to cover a quilt completely, or as a background "filler" to set off fancier motifs (see Feathered Heart Wall Hanging, pages 132–143). On a full-sized quilt it is hard to determine how far apart to make the rows and still come out even. The answer is to measure, calculate how many rows you'll need, and be prepared to make minor adjustments as you are close to finishing.

CURVED LINES

Curved lines can be stitched in several ways. Soft, undulating lines can be quilted in a channel or grid format using the quilting bar accessory (Diagram 3). The long curved line on the edge of this page is a pattern to help you get started. Traditional filler patterns created by intersecting circles, such as the Teacup (Diagrams 4-A and 4-B) and the Clamshell (Diagram 4-C), must be completely marked. For best results mark accurately and stitch with your machine's even-feed attachment, not in circles, but in a weaving curved line as shown. Consistency is important, but irregularity in a curved pattern is still less noticeable than in a straight-line geometric pattern.

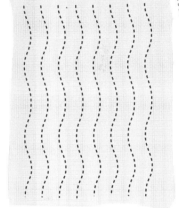

Diagram 3

Diagram 4

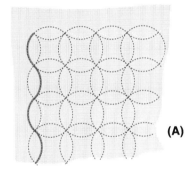

(A)

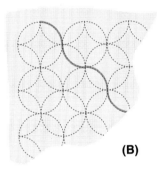

(B)

(C)

The next project shows you how to mark and stitch a teacup pattern on a pillow sham. The circle used for marking the pillow sham is 3⅝ inches in diameter. (Circles smaller than 2½ inches are too tight for machine-guided stitching but are fine for free-motion quilting. We'll get to that in Chapter 7.) Remember, practice makes perfect; don't put unnecessary expectations on your early machine-quilting projects. You're bound to have several pillows on your bed, and if your finished sham has a few mistakes, it can always go to the back of the stack.

Teacup Pillow Sham

SIZE
20 × 26 inches

MATERIALS REQUIRED
¾ yard of fabric for sham top
¾ yard of batting
¾ yard of lining fabric
⅝ yard of backing fabric
⅝ yard of fabric for ruffle
2⅝ yards of 2¼-inch gathered eyelet

Tradition has it that teacups were the right size and readily available for tracing around, hence the name of this pattern. Standard-sized pillows are 20 by 26 inches; king-sized pillows are 20 by 36 inches. Since pillow sizes and plumpness vary, please measure your pillows. Measure the circumference of your pillow and the length of your pillow from end to end. Pillow shams usually look best with a snug fit. The fabric requirements are for one 20- by 26-inch sham.

Although most projects in this book call for a ¼-inch seam allowance, because of the wear and tear associated with inserting and removing a pillow from its sham, ½-inch seam allowances are used for this project.

Cutting the Fabric

1. Cut one piece each from fabric for the sham top, batting, and lining 24 inches long by 30 inches wide. (Cut the 24-inch length along the selvage.) These will be trimmed to perfect size after layering and quilting.
2. For the back of the pillow, cut one piece 21 inches long by 22 inches wide and one piece 21 inches long by 12 inches wide. (Cut the 21-inch length along the selvage.) The two pieces will be used to make a lap-backed closure on the pillow.

Quilting the Teacups

Marking the Pattern   To mark the pattern

1. Look closely to notice the difference. Depending on the position of the marks on the circle and the way the circles overlap, the resulting shapes are either vertical and horizontal (Figure A-1) or diagonal (Figure A-2). The pillow sham was marked like Diagram 4-A, with five circles (about 3½ inches in diameter; see pattern on page 104) down and seven across filling a rectangle approximately 14 by 19 inches.
2. Draw a corner as in Figure B. The first circle has two sides touching the corner. The subsequent circles overlap as shown. Fill in empty arcs with partial circles.

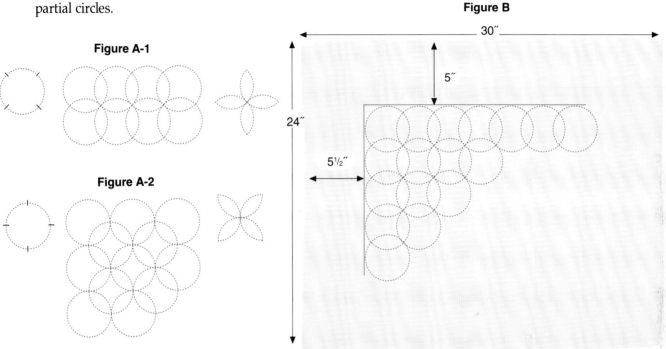

Figure A-1

Figure A-2

Figure B

Layering and Quilting   To layer and quilt the sham

1. Lay the backing, wrong side up, on a flat surface. Top with the batting, and center the sham top right side up on the batting. Pin baste to hold the layers in place.
2. Quilt the circles with vertical and horizontal gentle curving lines as shown in Diagram 4-A. It will actually take four different rows of quilting to make each circle. Stitch the borders around the circles.
3. Mark and trim the quilted sham top to 21 by 27 inches so that the quilted design is centered. The trimmed size includes ½-inch seam allowances.

Making the Ruffle

1. Cut three strips of fabric 7 inches wide by 45 inches long, lengthwise along the selvage. Piece the strips together to make one long strip.
2. Turn under and stitch a ¼-inch hem at each end of the strip to finish the raw edges.
3. Press the strip in half lengthwise, wrong sides facing and raw edges even.
4. Using a ¼-inch seam allowance, gather the ruffle strip to 96½ inches long.

Adding the Eyelet and Ruffle to the Sham Top

1. Layer the eyelet and the sham top, right sides facing and raw edges even. Pin in position, overlapping ends along one side.
2. Layer the ruffle on top of the eyelet, overlapping the ends with the eyelet ends. Baste in position through all layers, removing pins from the eyelet as you baste.

Finishing the Sham

1. Turn under and press a doubled 1-inch hem along one 21-inch side of each sham back. Stitch close to the inner pressed edge.
2. With right sides up, lap the hemmed edges of the sham backs 1½ inches. Baste upper and lower edges together (Figure C).
3. Layer the quilted, ruffled sham top and the lapped sham back with right sides facing and raw edges even. Sew all around the outside edges, using a ½-inch seam allowance. Trim diagonally across the corners to remove some of the bulk in the seam allowance.
4. Turn the sham right side out through the lapped back opening.

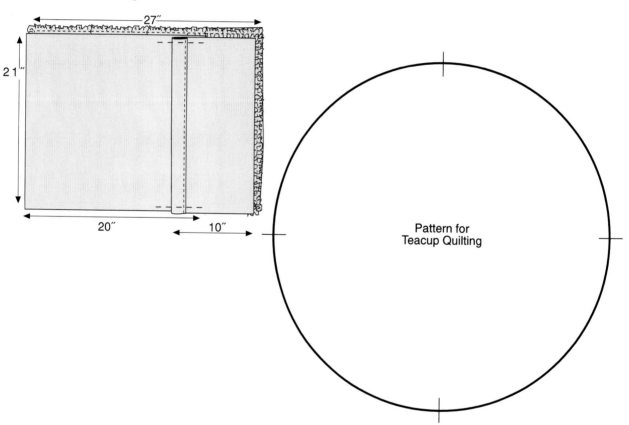

Figure C

Pattern for
Teacup Quilting

Marking a Clamshell

To mark a clamshell start with a baseline at the bottom of the design area. With the circle template notches in the 12, 3, 6, and 9 o'clock positions, place 3 and 9 on the line and draw the top half of the circle, as in Diagram 4-C. On subsequent rows, points 3 and 9 should touch the 12 o'clock (center top) positions of the previous row.

CABLES AND OTHER CONTINUOUS LINES

Cables and similar continuous-line designs selected for machine-guided quilting must be simple, with a minimum of turns in order to keep going in the same general direction. (Once you start free-motion quilting, the design possibilities will open up, but you will lose the neat, even stitch of "feed dogs up.")

Traditional cable quilting designs sold as stencils are often suitable for machine quilting. In the hand-quilted version of a traditional cable, the stitching creates a definite over and under design (Diagram 5). In the machine-quilted version, the lines continue unbroken, creating a pleasing "argyle"-type intersection instead (Diagram 6). You can adapt similar cable designs simply by continuing the lines in the "hidden" section.

CHOOSING A STENCIL

Plastic quilter's stencils are worth using when you want to mark a design on the surface of a quilt repeatedly and accurately. The narrow-cut section of the stencil guides the marker, while the solid area protects the quilt from stray marks. Extremely long cuts are broken up by bridges, or small connecting areas, that keep the stencil from falling apart. If you want a completely continuous line, it will be necessary to go back and fill in the areas you missed because of the bridges.

Precut stencils are readily available in quilt and fabric shops, but you'll find a much larger selection at quilt shows where stencil companies exhibit and by mail order. About the only complaint that cut stencils receive is that if you've found an 8-inch design you love, your block is invariably 7 inches, which is why you should at least know how to make a stencil.

MAKING YOUR OWN STENCILS

To make your own stencil, draw the design actual size and mark bridges so that there are no free-floating solid areas. Trace the design onto the stencil template material (usually translucent plastic or Mylar film) and cut it with an art knife. Take care not to cut away the bridges. Cutting is made easier and more accurate if you use a double-bladed knife, which lets you cut both edges of the channel simultaneously. Another tool, similar to a wood-burning device, is used with a special plastic material to make quilting stencils.

Once your stencil is cut, practice marking the design on newsprint. That way you can confirm how long the repeat is, practice turning a corner, and figure out how to stretch or squeeze a design to fit into a certain space before you start marking your fabric.

If you really want to incorporate motif designs available in stencil form, it is time to learn free-motion quilting.

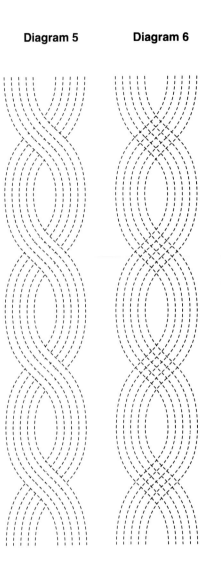

Diagram 5   **Diagram 6**

Hand Quilting   Machine Continuous Quilting

7

FEED DOGS DOWN: FREE-MOTION QUILTING

LEARNING TO TAKE CONTROL

Free-motion quilting is the skill that will make your machine-quilting repertoire complete. It is common for people to put off trying free-motion quilting, but once they have tried it, they frequently don't want to do anything else! This is because they have discovered the incredible versatility it allows.*

Free motion means just that: You can quilt in any direction. In practical terms, you don't have to turn an entire quilt around and continue stitching forward the way you do when the feed dogs are up, pushing the fabric under the needle. With the feed dogs down, the machine provides the power for the needle to move up and down, but you determine how fast the needle moves and when and in what direction to move the fabric. A stitch is made whenever the needle enters the fabric. The speed of the needle and the pace with which you move the fabric determine the stitch size and consistency. In many ways the technique combines machine embroidery and quilting.

The positive way to look at free-motion quilting is to say it allows you complete control. The negative way is to say that you must take control! Or, as the saying goes, "With freedom goes responsibility."

Get Ready with Some Practice Stitches

As described in Chapter 2, free-motion quilting is usually done with the darning foot attached and the feed dogs down or covered (page 19). When I'm working on a project, I always layer little scraps of fabric and batting together, and every time I am ready to start free-motion quilting, I do some sample stitching on the scrap. It makes sense to check the tension and make sure I like the thread color, but for the most part I like to reestablish the eye–hand–foot relationship before I start on the real project.

Layer a scrap of fabric with batting and backing; then jump in and practice. Use invisible thread or cotton thread that matches the predominant color in the fabric. Your actual stitches are much less visible with nylon thread, but you'll have less tension difficulty with cotton thread. Remember to loosen your upper tension if you are using nylon thread.

Hold the area where you are stitching taut and keep the fabric moving at a fairly calm, steady pace. The hardest thing to believe is that the faster you sew, the easier it is to do, but keeping the

*See Chapter 9, where we reprint Hari Walner's wonderful handout sheet "Overcoming the Fear of Free-Motion Quilting." The advice she gives there is invaluable.

needle moving fast seems to be the surest way to achieve a regular stitch length. (Of course, you can go too fast. If your stitches are very tiny, you are either stitching too fast or moving too slowly.) Remember, the stitches will never be uniform in length the way they are when the feed dogs and needle are synchronized. It may sound complicated, but it really isn't. Begin by moving the fabric in any direction—write your name, make loops, do anything—just allow the stitches to develop.

After you've been stitching for awhile, you will notice that puckers are most likely whenever two lines of stitching cross. To reduce puckering and create a nice quilted effect, try to develop a random motion that curves forward and back, and then cuts back again without actually crossing a previous stitching line. (This is a suggestion, not a commandment.) With just a little practice you'll be amazed at the results. When this random stitching is done tightly or very close together, it is called *stippling* (see page 109).

Machine and Body Position

Free-motion quilting can make tremendous demands on your arms and body. I like to work with my machine set into a table so that the bed of the machine is level with the tabletop. If that is not possible for you, at least get your body high enough so that your forearms can rest comfortably on the edge of the table. An adjustable secretarial chair with the sewing machine at computer table height might do the trick. Essentially, you want to avoid having to hold your arms up, and you want to position your eyes so you can see where and what you are stitching. I use a mid-height stool, which raises the height of my torso but still allows me to rest my feet on the floor.

Hand Position I see lots of people free-motion quilting with both hands on top of the fabric, basically pushing their fabric around. This position is fine for in-the-ditch quilting when the machine is pulling the fabric. It may even work for other people when they do free-motion quilting, but it doesn't work for me!

My left hand is always *under* the layered fabric—I just grab it from the back. It creates a slight bunching, but I never hold it in one place long enough to wrinkle. Meanwhile, my right hand rolls up the edge and grabs it so that my hands are about 6 inches apart. Then I pull the fabric between my hands just enough to be taut. Most of the time, the fabric is actually raised off the surface of the machine, so that the "drag" resulting from friction is reduced to a minimum. This position is easier with blocks and border strips than it is with full-sized quilts, but I do it with quilts too.

A Few Safety Tips

The end of the darning foot attachment does not actually touch the fabric, but floats just above the surface. Its purpose is to hold down the fabric when the force of the emerging needle tries to pull it up. In addition, the darning foot is a perpetual marker of exactly where the needle is going to go down. Sometimes, when you are moving the fabric around near the needle, it is easy to

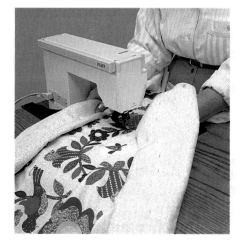

An elevated position not only allows comfortable seating, with one's feet on the floor, but provides a clear view of the quilt.

lose track of the exact needle position. The foot helps out by telling you where you want the fabric to be and where you don't want your fingers to be.

If you have long hair, pull it back when you're at the machine. In the rush of doing so many things at once, you can let your head get too close to the take-up lever and your hair can get caught.

MORE ABOUT CONTINUOUS CURVES

Our discussion on continuous curves started in Chapter 5, where we discussed machine-guided quilting with the feed dogs up. There we had to stitch in a set pattern and direction all the way across the quilt. Putting the feed dogs down changes the picture entirely. You'll find that stitching back and forth inside a patchwork block or border is very easy with free-motion quilting, as are the Teacup and Clamshell fillers. Not only are they easier to do, but you could even try them in smaller sizes. Your success, however, still rests on how clever you are at creating stitching sequences, a subject that could take a book in itself. (See Resources, page 202, for Barbara Johannah's books.)

MEANDERING

Meandering is a random, generally flowing, curving-back-and-forth quilting style. It is open, rather than dense, and leaves fairly large areas unquilted. It is important to keep the density of quilting balanced throughout the project. If more dense quilting were added to adjacent areas, there is a good chance the quilt would draw up and pucker.

Meandering makes a perfect border finish for a piece that has been quilted in the ditch. My first in-the-ditch quilts used bonded

Meandering among the flowers on a print fabric accentuates the shapes and colors while randomly filling in the background.

medium-weight polyester batting, and it was possible to leave 4-
to 6-inch sections unquilted (even more if the quilts didn't get
hard wear). Because I was still minimizing the amount of quilting
that showed on the surface of the quilt, I left many of my borders
unquilted. Now that amount of space looks empty to me and I am
going back and adding meandering quilting to many of those borders. It is easy, fast, and effective.

Quite often the fabric will give you guidance for the quilting
pattern. Just meander in the background of a print or move from
flower to flower. You can use invisible thread or a matching color.
Because puckers on the back of the quilt are most likely to happen
when one row of machine quilting crosses another, it makes sense
not to meander back and forth across previous stitching. Avoid
loops and circles; instead reverse your direction in sweeping
turns, not harsh angles.

Stippling fills the background more densely and evenly.

STIPPLING

A stipple stitch in hand quilting is a very fine, dense, random
stitch, generally used to fill and hold down a background area
around a motif of some kind. Free-motion stipple quilting by machine is a dream. The stipple stitch covers the area in an evenly
dense, convoluted pattern. The stitching lines can be very tight
(less than ¼ inch apart) or a little more open. Much more than ½
inch apart and you are beginning to meander instead of stipple.

The next project was inspired by a postal stamp design. If the
full quilt seems overly ambitious, an individual block would make
a lovely pillow or could be sewn into a charming tote bag. By alternating the stippling between baskets and background, a
positive/negative coloration is achieved that could be equally effective on other mirror image patterns. This project provides great
stipple practice.

Selecting the Thread

Thread Type and Size   The wonderful variety of decorative threads available is enough to make a strong heart pound. Sulky® size 30 rayon embroidery thread was selected for this quilt because of its easy use, high luster, rich colors, and general availability. The colors used were 1042, 1079, 1090, 1122, and 1192. When possible, the heavier size 30 thread was used, but color was a more important criterion than weight in the baskets, since they were very tightly stippled. At press time, colors 1079 and 1192 were only available in size 40. The colors used in the border were 1090 and 1122, both size 30.

Color   While the quilt could have been done in only one color of thread for a more traditional whole-cloth quilt look, the assorted strong colors seemed more interesting for photography. Pastel colors would give a much softer, almost frosted look. Before committing to any thread, stitch a large enough sample to be confident you will like the choice.

Cost   Before you reject this quilt because the price of decorative threads is more than you are used to paying for thread, consider. The extra cost of thread is more than balanced by the ease of selection and generally lower price of muslin or solid-color broadcloth. In addition, you buy less fabric for this quilt because there is so little piecing. Remember, the time you are investing deserves the best thread you can afford.

Cutting the Fabric

Cut twenty 15½-inch squares from muslin or broadcloth, twenty 15½-inch squares of backing fabric, and twenty 15½-inch squares of batting. The finished block size is 14 inches, so the blocks will be trimmed to a perfect 14½-inch size after quilting, but before the blocks are joined.

Tracing the Pattern

The basket pattern provided is for one-fourth of the complete block. To make the complete pattern on paper, trace the design; then rotate the pattern 90 degrees, matching dotted lines. Trace the next one-fourth of the design. Rotate and trace twice more to complete the pattern.

When you are using light-color solid fabric for quilt blocks, simply center the fabric block right side up on top of the completed pattern and trace the pattern with a water-erasable marking pen.

1. Find the center point of each of the twenty blocks and mark a " + " with lines parallel to each side and intersecting at the center point.

2. Align the center point and placement lines of the pattern with the " + " on each fabric block.

SIZE

85 × 99 inches
Block Size: 14 inches square

MATERIALS REQUIRED

8⅝ yards muslin or solid-color broadcloth for blocks and border

1,000 yards of cotton or cotton-wrapped polyester thread to match backing fabric

Rayon embroidery thread* (see Selecting the Thread)

⅝ yard fabric for French-fold binding

8⅝ yards backing fabric, including finishing strips

6 yards medium-weight bonded polyester, or king-sized packaged batting

Metal ruler or straight edge

Water-erasable marking pen

*Size 30 Sulky® thread was used for most of this project. Each 130-yard spool was enough to complete two blocks. Two spools each of five colors was enough to complete four blocks of each color. The ribbon border will require two additional spools of each color and three or four of the white.

TIP: Grain Line When Marking

On quilts with large sections of light-colored or white background, grain line direction is often visible. To prevent any problem, mark the squares with the lengthwise grain on the vertical, going up and down. Mark the upper left square of each block so the basket, not the background, is stippled (see Figure A-1 on page 115). That way, when the blocks are put together, the grain line direction will be consistent.

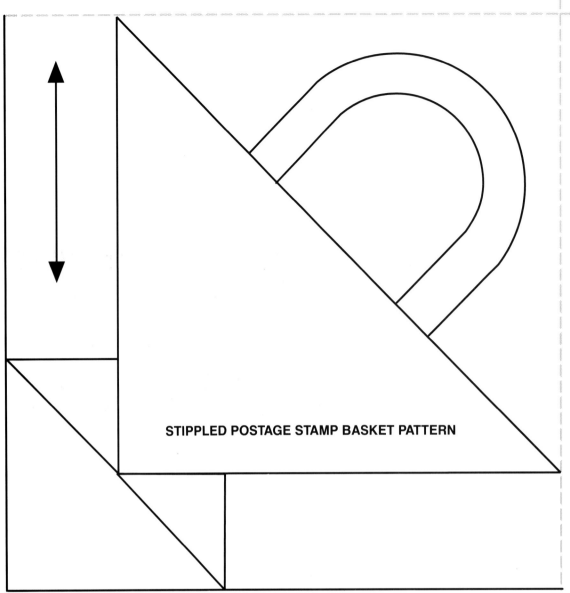

STIPPLED POSTAGE STAMP BASKET PATTERN

¹⁄₄ of Block - actual size

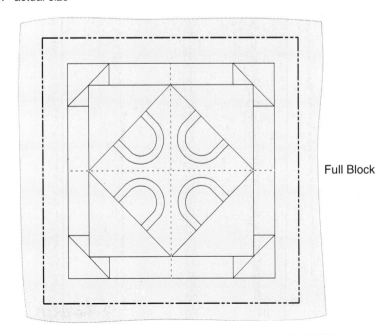

Full Block

112

STIPPLED POSTAGE STAMP BASKET BLOCK

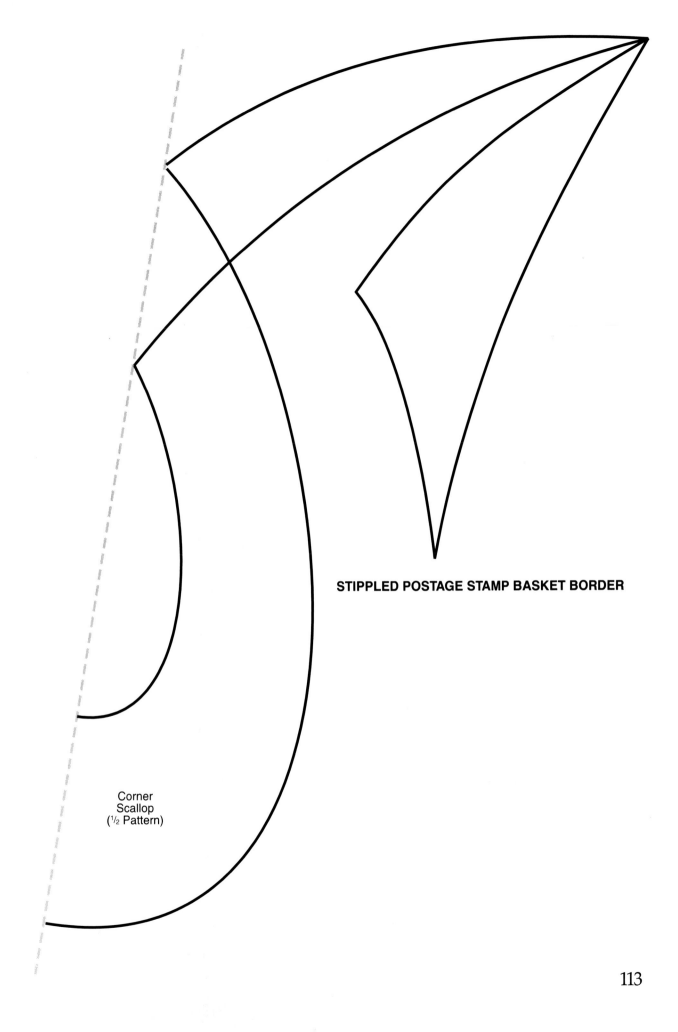

STIPPLED POSTAGE STAMP BASKET BORDER

Corner
Scallop
(¹/₂ Pattern)

113

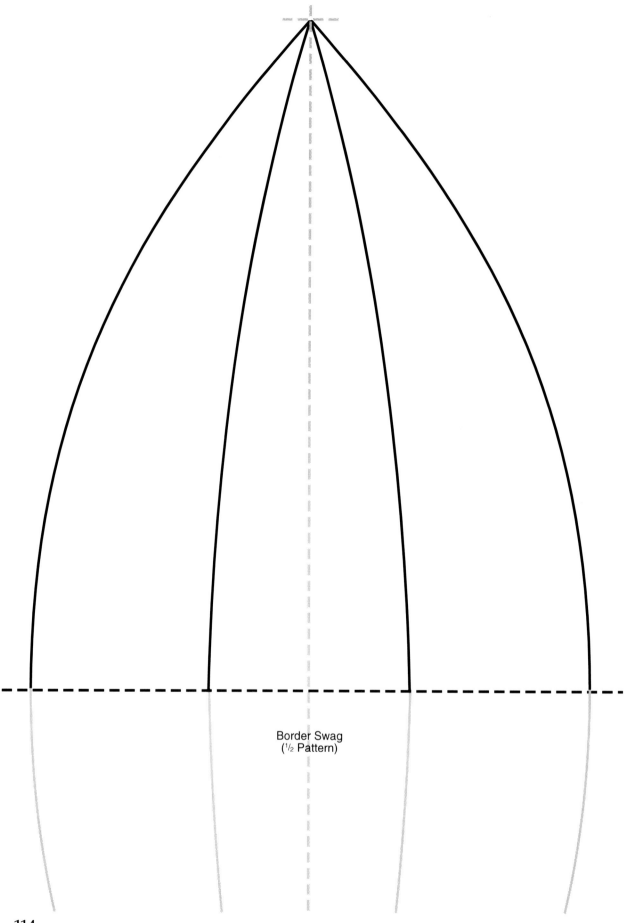

Border Swag
(1/2 Pattern)

Quilting the Design

1. Layer each quilt block with batting and backing. Use pins or basting to hold the layers in place. When quilting the design, it is helpful to adjust your chair higher than usual, to be able to look down on the marking and stitch more accurately.

2. Straight-stitch all design lines, using continuous stitching as much as possible. When stitching the basket handle, use smaller stitches to curve more gracefully.

   To create continuous quilting it occasionally makes good sense to repeat stitching on the same line. When you do that, try to stitch directly on top of the first line of stitching.

3. Stipple-quilt inside the design area, creating the positive/negative effect. Try to plan your quilting so that you can move from one section to the next at a point where you have already done straight-line quilting (Figure A-2).

4. Remove water-erasable marking before assembling.

Assembling the Blocks into Rows

1. Before assembling the blocks, trim each block to 14½ inches square, which includes ¼-inch seam allowances. This is done most easily with a large square acrylic ruler and the rotary cutter.

2. Lay out the blocks in the order desired, in five horizontal rows of four blocks. Be sure that the positive/negative design is oriented correctly for all baskets (Figure B). That is, all blocks should have either a stippled basket or a stippled background in the upper left corner. Mark the position on each block, Row 1–Block A, Row 2–Block A, and so on (Figure C).

3. Because the stitching does not go to the edge of the blocks, they can be joined without the finishing strips used on the Virginia Reel Quilt.

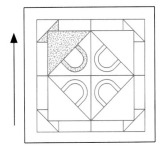

Figure A-1

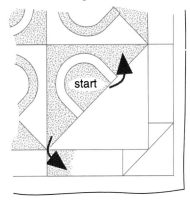

Figure A-2

Figure B

Figure C

Figure D

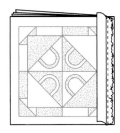

Figure E

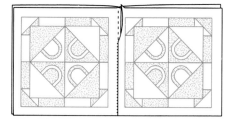

Figure F

14¼"

7¼"

2¼"

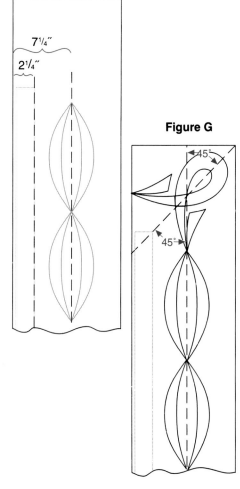

Figure G

Quilt-As-You-Sew Block Assembly Without Finishing Strips

1. Pick up the first two blocks in Row 1. Place these blocks with right sides facing. Make sure the center lines match. Pull back the top layer of fabric, which is the backing fabric of the top block. Stitch through the remaining five layers of fabric and batting (Figure D). Trim away the excess batting in the seam allowance.

2. In the same way, join all of the blocks in each horizontal row.

3. Secure the loose edges of backing in each row. Turn under the edge of loose backing fabric ¼ inch, so that it is even with the stitching line where the blocks were joined together (Figure E). Slip-stitch the folded edge in place directly on top of the seam line, using the seam line as an anchor and a guide when stitching.

If the blocks were trimmed accurately, the seam allowance will be exactly ¼ inch. Do not turn under more than a ¼-inch seam allowance, because this will create a ripple on the top side of the quilt block.

Joining the Rows

Finishing strips are used to sew the five rows of blocks to each other. (See the Virginia Reel Quilt, Joining the Rows, page 61, for details.) Cut four strips of fabric 1½ inches wide by 59 inches long. When the quilt interior is completed, it should measure 56½ inches by 70½ inches, including ¼-inch seam allowances.

Cutting and Marking the Borders

The border for this quilt finishes to 14 inches and is quilted before being added. This method is discussed in detail in Chapter 11.

1. From border fabric, cut two strips 14½ inches by 70½ inches for sides and two each of 14¼ inches by 84½ inches for top and bottom. These lengths are mathematically correct. It is, however, especially important to measure your quilt and make any necessary adjustments when the borders are being quilted separately. Cut batting and backing strips the same length, but 16 inches wide.

2. On each border fabric lightly draw two straight lines. The first one should be 2¼ inches, and the second one 7¼ inches from one long edge (Figure F).

3. Center the double scallop on the second line and transfer the pattern to the right side of the border fabric in the same way that you marked the baskets (Figure F). Match the dotted lines and connect end to end, positioning five scallops along side borders and four scallops centered along top and bottom borders.

4. The corner scallop design is marked on the top and bottom borders. The center line of the design follows a 45-degree angle from the marked center line of the border. Match the dotted lines and connect the ends with the double scallops, making adjustments as necessary (Figure G).

Quilting and Adding the Borders

1. Layer the fabric according to page 87. Begin by quilting the straight lines along the side. Next quilt the edges of the double scallop and stipple-quilt the scallop interior. Finally, loosely stipple-quilt around the double scallop. (This is not as loose as a meandering stitch or nearly as tight as a stipple.)

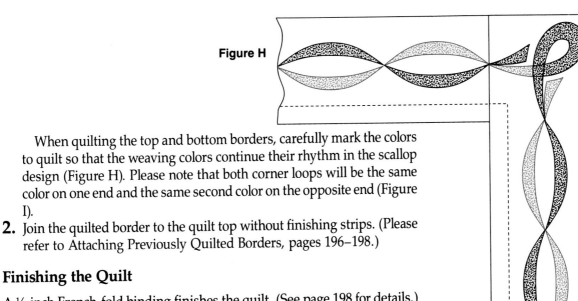

Figure H

    When quilting the top and bottom borders, carefully mark the colors to quilt so that the weaving colors continue their rhythm in the scallop design (Figure H). Please note that both corner loops will be the same color on one end and the same second color on the opposite end (Figure I).

2. Join the quilted border to the quilt top without finishing strips. (Please refer to Attaching Previously Quilted Borders, pages 196–198.)

Finishing the Quilt

A ½-inch French-fold binding finishes the quilt. (See page 198 for details.)

Figure I

QUILTED PICTURES

Meandering and stippling are attractive, easy, and effective uses of free-motion quilting. The next two projects provide a hint of the flexibility, precision, and realism free-motion techniques contribute to machine quilting. Your sewing machine needle could be considered an electric pencil, and free motion lets you move that "pencil" anywhere you like. Picture quilts with lots of lines going in different directions are easy to complete using free-motion quilting.

Blowing in the Wind

Selecting the Fabric

This wall hanging is a softer interpretation of the classic mythical North Wind character. The white-on-muslin star print fabric seems well suited for personifying the blowing wind on a starry summer night. The gold lamé border and piping add sparkle without distracting from the machine-quilting design.

Cutting the Fabric

Cut a 36-inch square from the muslin print fabric for the center square. The finished size is 30 inches, so the square will be trimmed to 30½ inches after quilting, before adding the borders.

Enlarging the Pattern with a Grid

The interior section of the quilt finishes to 30 inches square. Each square in the pattern grid represents a 2-inch square. The face pattern included is full-sized and fits into a rectangle on the scale drawing.

1. Use paper large enough to accommodate the full-sized pattern, and with a ruler and pencil, draw horizontal and vertical lines necessary to create the 2-inch squares.

2. Square by square, draw the original pattern onto the larger grid. Trace the face pattern into the rectangular opening. Draw lightly first. Smooth out curves and refine lines. When satisfied, make the lines heavy enough to see through the fabric.

Tracing the Pattern

Place the center fabric square, right side up, on top of the pattern. Trace the design. Mark as lightly as possible, yet strong enough to be visible while quilting.

Layering and Quilting

1. Cut batting and backing to 2 inches bigger all around than the finished size of the wall hanging, or approximately 44 inches by 44 inches.

2. Place the backing, wrong side up, on top of a smooth, flat surface. Layer the batting on top of the backing, and center the marked square on top of both layers. Pin or baste the layers together.

3. There are several inches of exposed backing and batting around the center square. Fold those sections in half so that the backing is on top and no batting is exposed. Pin in place. This covers the exposed batting so that it won't get caught while quilting and reduces the size of the project.

4. Quilt in any order you choose. I did several of the longer, straighter lines with the straight-stitch and even-feed attachment. Because the straight lines are spread across the quilt, stitching them first served the purpose of more secure basting for the free-motion work I did next. Finally, complete the face and hair (or is it clouds?).

The hair/clouds provided lots of opportunity for free-thinking free-motion work. My decision was mostly to echo-quilt, but to break the echo pattern just enough with a different contour to prevent boredom.

5. Mark a line around the completely quilted top 30½ inches square, which includes ¼-inch seam allowances. This is done most easily with a large acrylic ruler. Do not cut anything yet!

SIZE
40 × 40 inches

MATERIALS REQUIRED

1 yard of white-on-muslin print fabric for center square

1¼ yards of fabric for backing

1¼ yards of batting

¼ yard of gold lamé fabric for first border, cut crosswise (if tissue lamé, you will also need fusible lightweight interfacing)

½ yard of muslin and white stripe fabric for second border, cut crosswise

4½ yards of ¼-inch purchased gold lamé piping

⅝ yard of white fabric for French-fold binding

Water-erasable marking pen

Decorative threads: size 30 rayon ecru and gold metallic

BLOWING IN THE WIND SCALE DRAWING

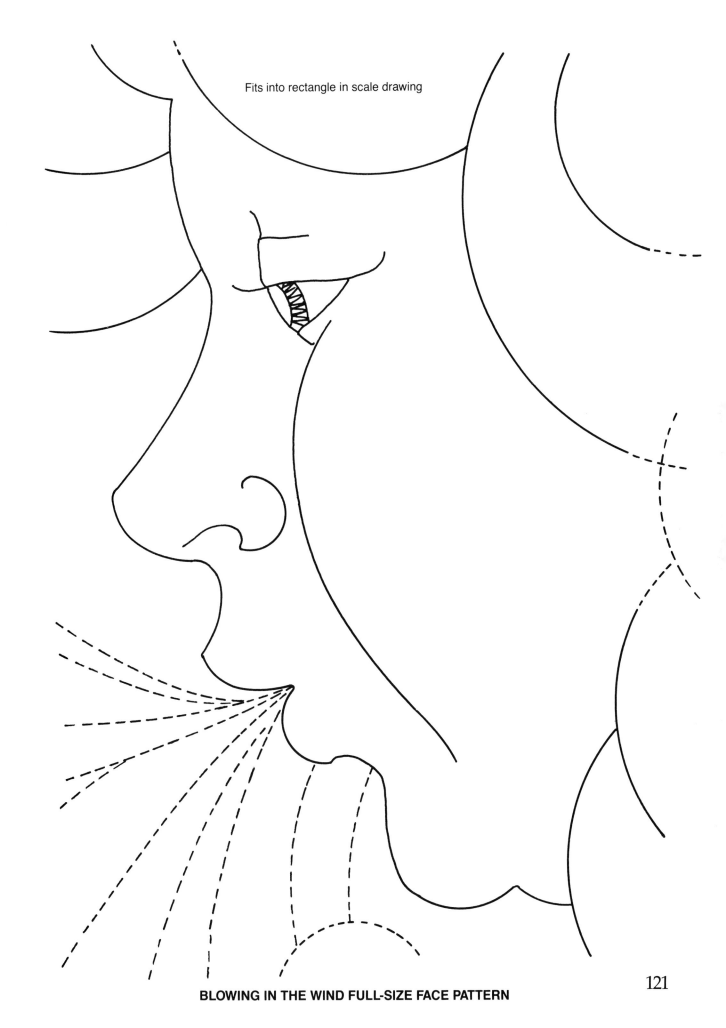

Fits into rectangle in scale drawing

BLOWING IN THE WIND FULL-SIZE FACE PATTERN

Adding the Borders The borders finish to 1 inch and 3 inches. If you are using tissue lamé for a border, stabilize it by fusing interfacing to the wrong side before cutting border strips.

Add both borders using the Modified Quilt-As-You-Sew method (page 196). Then trim away the excess fabric from the center square. Do not cut batting or backing. The strip pieces for the second border were cut crosswise, so that the stripes would be perpendicular to the quilt. Because the corners are mock mitered (page 191), strip pieces must be cut at least 38½ inches long.

Adding the Piping Add purchased ¼-inch piping to the outside edge of the second border according to the package directions, using a zipper foot on your sewing machine. Instead of trying to turn the corners of the quilt with the piping, cut and sew piping to the two sides of the quilt, and then to the top and bottom.

Finishing the Quilt

A ⅝-inch French-fold binding finishes the quilt. (Refer to page 198 for details.) If desired, add a sleeve for hanging the quilt to display.

This design is adapted from a challenge quilt I made several years ago. I selected the blowing motif to coordinate with the subtle leaf design on the fabrics. As you can see, the quilting effort, although fun and instructive (I experimented with 14 different threads), was wasted on the busy background–or perhaps you can't see, which proves the point even more!

SPLIT-SURFACE STITCHING AND STABILIZING

Free-motion quilting is the technique most commonly used by machine quilters to stitch demanding designs. However, for projects with very dense stitching that borders on embroidery, a slightly different method is recommended. Instead of layering fabric with batting and backing, the majority of the stitching is worked on the surface layer only. To prevent the force of the sewing machine needle from pushing the fabric into the needle hole, the fabric is stabilized with a lightweight interfacing or by pulling it taut in an embroidery hoop. To help prevent fabric distortion, you replace your machine's zigzag plate with the single-hole plate. But don't forget to change the plate back before doing a zigzag or decorative stitch or you will break the needle.

There are no rights and wrongs to the next project, just plenty of options. Called Quilter's Nonshedding Pine, it features machine-quilted pine needles, stenciled pinecones, and a dimensional wired ribbon bow, all mounted on a Foamcore™ base. It is designed to go over a doorway, so you don't have to be overly concerned about mistakes. How many people do you know who will be eye level with that? This is where machine embroidery and machine quilting really begin to cross over.

Quilter's Nonshedding Pine

9 × 29 inches

MATERIALS REQUIRED

¾ yard ecru background and backing
    fabric
12- × 32-inch piece of batting
Water-erasable marking pen
Assorted green threads for quilting
Brown thread for quilting
Optional: brown fabric dye
    dark brown or black fabric paint pen
    stencil brush
    stencil acrylic and art knife
Optional: gold quilting thread and/or
    paint
1½ yards 2-inch-wide wired ribbon
Foamcore™ for mounting form
Appropriate knife for cutting
    Foamcore
Thick craft glue
20- × 30-inch piece of cotton or thin
    polyester batting
Optional: 2¼ yards of cording for
    outside edge

Making the Pattern

The pattern in the book is for the left half and is in two sections (see pages 126 and 127). To make a full pattern, trace two complete halves. To create the right half, turn one half over and retrace on the second side of the paper. Vary the position of a few branches on the second side for a more natural look and add the fifth pinecone to one branch at the center (see photograph). Then tape the halves together.

TIP: Stabilizing Surface Fabric

There are several ways to stabilize a surface fabric for machine appliqué or heavy machine quilting.

1. Tear-away background stabilizer: This looks like a nonwoven interfacing but actually tears away from the stitches. This type of stabilizer tears away better on appliqué than a quilting design like this.
2. Solvy™: This is the brand name for a water-soluble background stabilizer, distributed by Sulky. Surely there are others, but this is the one of which I am aware. It has a filmlike look and dissolves in water when stitching is complete.
3. Machine embroidery hoops: These are especially designed so that they will fit under the presser foot and the fabric will be flat on the machine surface. Ask for these where sewing machines are sold. They only hold a small area at one time and need to be moved frequently.
4. Lightweight nonwoven interfacing: In some projects, such as this, the layer of interfacing that is not going to be removed could be used to stabilize the surface fabric. The extra weight and crispness of the interfacing are not so terribly obtrusive, and indeed are a benefit.

Marking and Stitching

Lightly mark the twig structure (Figure A-1). Mark only as many little pine needles as you think are necessary. The stitching will only use those lines as a guide, not actually follow them. Stitch pine needles first, on the top fabric only. Layer with batting and backing just when you are ready to do the last color of green needles and the brown spines. The final stitching will adequately secure the three layers together and provide enough quilting dimension.

Figure A-1

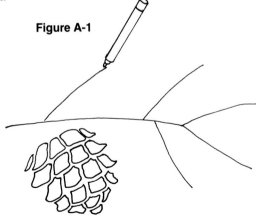

Thread Selection and Practice Stitching

The fabric selection on this project is easy, a nice ecru background fabric. The thread selection can be very simple, a couple of greens and a brown. However, if you are a thread collector, this is a place where you can show off. Pull out every green, including the metallics.

Practice on a small sample of fabric, prepared with your stabilizer of choice. If you are using several different greens, the idea is to layer the colors doing staggered portions in each color. As the colors build, it creates a more natural look with more depth. If you have a gold metallic, or a variegated metallic including gold, include that for a glint of sunshine. A dark blue-green gives good contrast. The thread used on this project is all from Sulky. The motion is an easy out and back, scoot up the spine, out and back again. Leave some space between needles on the first color and fill in as you repeat with additional colors (Figures A-2, A-3). Vary the length of the pine needles, similar to the pattern, by varying how far out you stitch.

In reality, because of the above-the-door placement, the detail of multiple colors will be appreciated more by you, as you stitch, than by anyone else. However, it is good practice, and you may decide you also want to make the pillow or collar variations, shown at the end of this section, where the detail is more visible.

Figure A-2

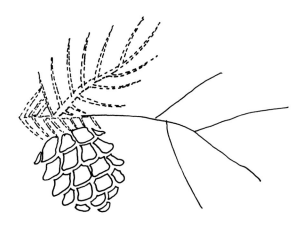

Figure A-3

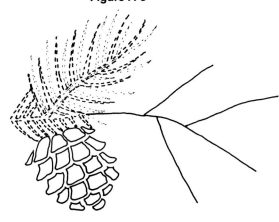

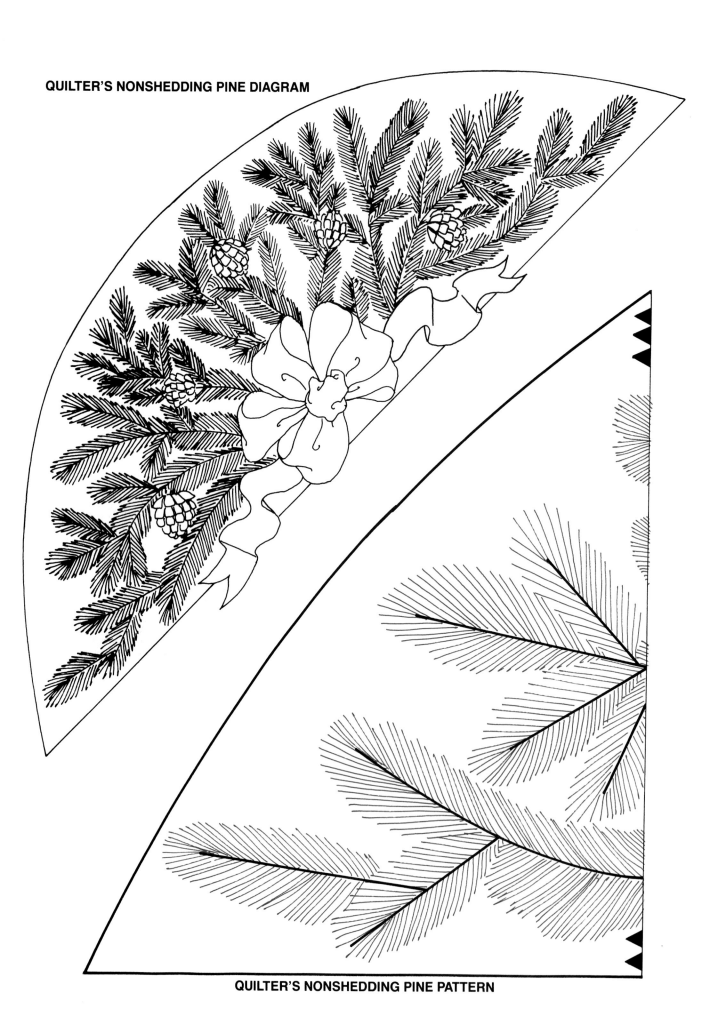

QUILTER'S NONSHEDDING PINE PATTERN

Match notches to complete pattern

Making the Pinecones with Optional Stenciling

The pinecones in the piece shown were stenciled (Figure B), but if you prefer, fill in those shapes with dense stitching. If you are not stenciling, skip to step 6.

1. Wash and press the background fabric.
2. Cut the stencil, making sure you leave enough surrounding acrylic to protect the fabric.
3. Stencil pinecones as positioned on pattern. To get a better feeling of dimension, stencil light sections as well as dark.
4. Add dark detail marks with a fabric paint pen, if desired (Figure B).
5. Heat set as directed on fabric dyes. Let fabric cool down.
6. When pinecones are complete, go back and use water-erasable marker to draw the spines of the pine (Figure A-1).
7. With the sample piece as your guide, quilt as you determined was most desirable.

Finishing Details

1. Cut Foamcore to shape with an art knife. Pad with one layer of batting that covers the front, wraps around the edges, and is glued in place on the back.
2. Wrap stitched piece in place around the Foamcore and glue down on back side.
3. Make or purchase wired ribbon bow and streamers.
4. Generally, the piece is expected to rest on a flat surface and lean against a wall, but depending on where and how you are using the pine, it may be necessary to add a ribbon loop at the center top to help make it more secure.

Nonshedding Pine Pillow and Collar Variations

If you have fallen in love with this process or just find either of these projects (Figures C and D) more suitable for you, Quilter's Nonshedding Pine would be very suitable on a sailor-type collar. These illustrations suggest how the pine pattern as printed could fit a typical sailor collar. The pillow is a free-form interpretation of the techniques.

MOTIF QUILTING

For many people free-motion quilting is all about being able to stitch traditional hand-quilting designs. Ideally, your designs should have continuous lines, but not every design you may want to machine-quilt will fall into this category. The only sensible way to stitch feathered designs, for example, is to double-stitch some sections. Be as accurate as possible, but don't go crazy. The loft of the batting usually conceals the discrepancy when the stitching lines don't exactly match.

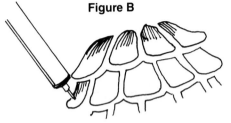

Figure B

Figure C

Figure D

Feathered Heart Pillow

The quilting on the pillow shown was actually machine-guided, as discussed on pages 99–101. Although machine-guided quilting can be very accurate, it is much slower than free-motion. Machine-guided quilting on a piece much larger than the pillow would be difficult because of the constant turning involved.

Cutting the Fabric

Use the pattern provided to cut the pillow top, batting, lining, and pillow back.

Quilting the Pillow

Mark the quilting pattern on the pillow top. Layer with batting and lining. Quilt using free-motion or machine-guided techniques.

Assembling the Pillow

The pillow is finished with a 1-inch purchased, pregathered lace strip and a 2¼-inch finished self-fabric ruffle. (See page 73, Making and Adding a Single Ruffle.)

1. Layer the pillow top and the lace right sides facing, raw edges even. Pin in position, overlapping the ends along one side. Layer the ruffle on top of the lace, overlapping the ends with the lace ends. Baste in position through all layers.
2. Place the pillow top and back right sides facing. Sew all around the outside edge, leaving an opening along one side for turning. Clip the corners of the seam allowance diagonally.
3. Turn the pillow right side out. Stuff tightly, pushing stuffing into the corners of the pillow. Slip-stitch the opening closed.

SIZE
15 × 18 inches

MATERIALS REQUIRED
1 yard of pink print fabric, including ruffle
18- × 22-inch piece of lining fabric
18- × 22-inch piece of quilt batting
1¼ yards of 1-inch-wide purchased, pregathered lace
Polyester filling

129

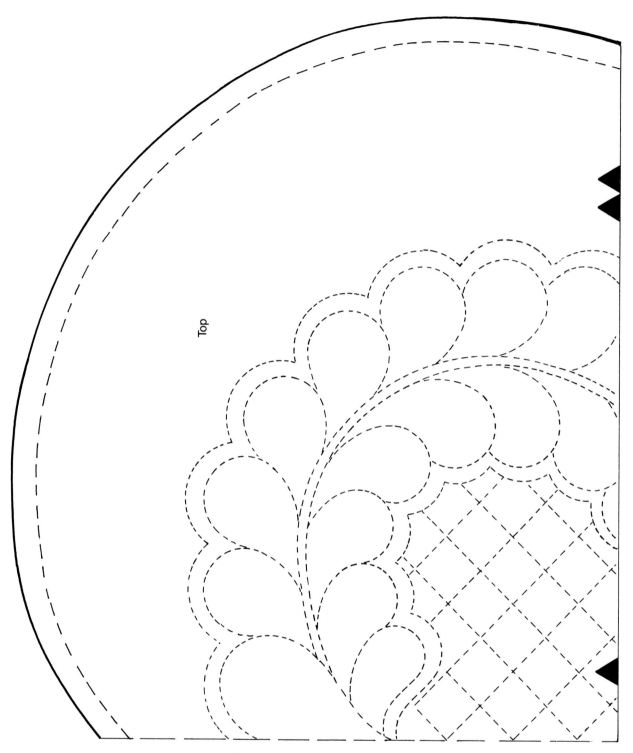

Top

FEATHERED HEART PILLOW PATTERN

130

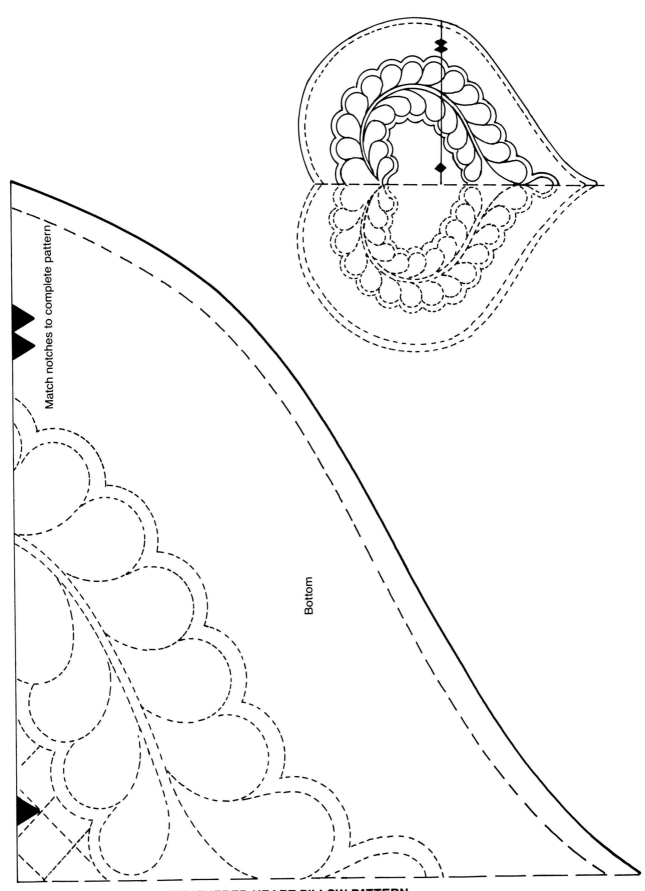

Match notches to complete pattern

Bottom

FEATHERED HEART PILLOW PATTERN

131

Feathered Heart Wall Hanging

Neutral fabrics were chosen for the Feathered Heart Wall Hanging to highlight the elaborate quilting. For easier construction the wall hanging is marked and quilted in individual units (five sections) (Figure A). The center section, with its large feathered heart and surrounding feathered heart border, is quilted first. The four corners are quilted separately and then sewn to the center using Quilt-As-You-Sew techniques.

Cutting the Fabric

1. Cut one 25-inch square each from muslin, backing, and batting for the center of the quilt top. The finished size of this section is 22½ inches.
2. Cut two 22-inch squares each from light brown fabric, backing, and batting for the corner sections. These will be cut in half diagonally after marking seam lines on the fabric squares.

Tracing the Pattern

Use the patterns provided to create the quilting design. Either make a stencil (page 105) or make a pattern to trace onto fabric using a light table. Trace the pattern with smooth, dark lines onto heavy white paper. Sections shown in dotted lines represent portions of the pattern that will be overlapped and should be copied as dots to prevent duplicating sections that should not be duplicated!

Marking the Center Square

See pages 96–98 for a discussion of marking fabric and using a light table. It is a good idea to practice marking the quilting design on paper first.

SIZE
34 × 34 inches

MATERIALS REQUIRED
1 yard of muslin or ecru fabric for quilt top center section and French-fold binding
1 yard of light brown fabric for corner sections
1⅜ yards of backing fabric
1⅜ yards of batting
Water-erasable marking pen
Sulky 30 weight decorative rayon thread (optional)

Figure A

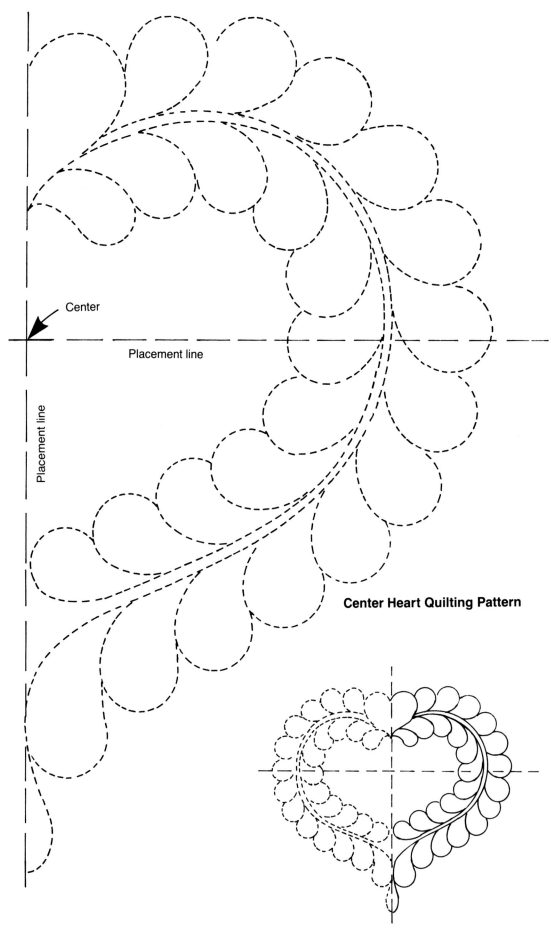

Center

Placement line

Placement line

Center Heart Quilting Pattern

FEATHERED HEART WALL HANGING

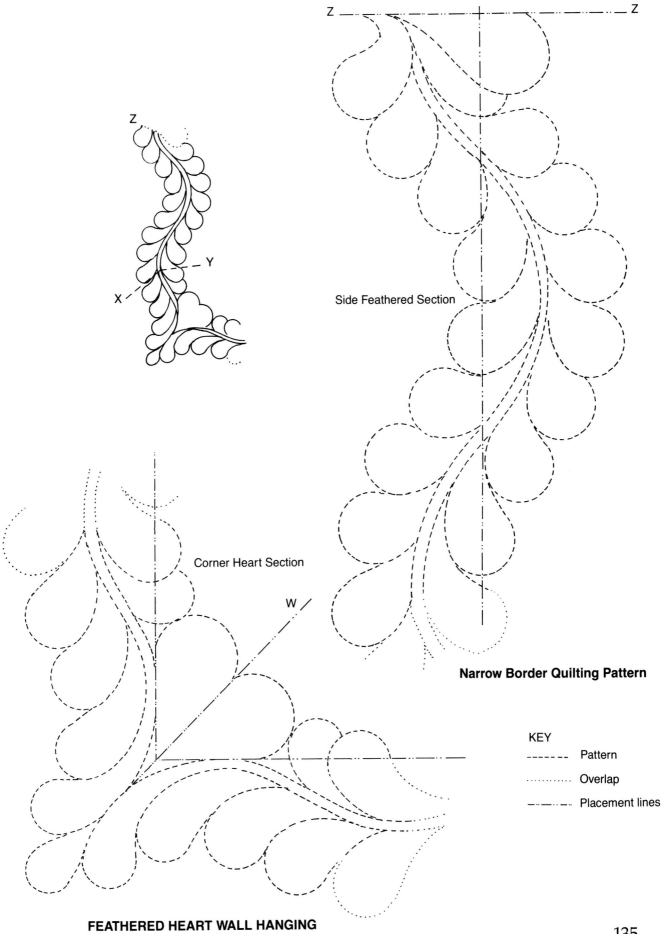

Side Feathered Section

Corner Heart Section

W

Z —————————————— Z

Z

X

Y

Narrow Border Quilting Pattern

KEY
- - - - - Pattern
· · · · · Overlap
—··—··— Placement lines

FEATHERED HEART WALL HANGING

135

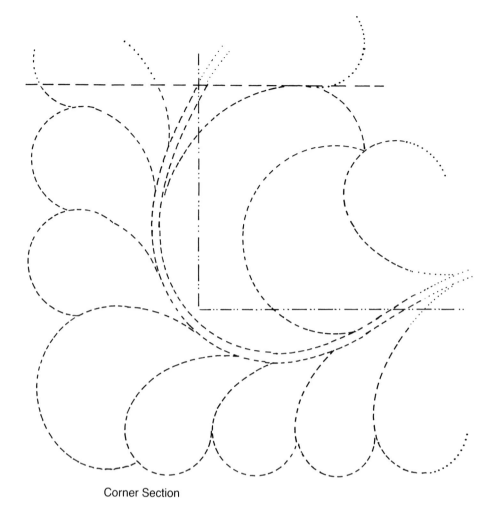

Corner Section

Wide Border Quilting Pattern

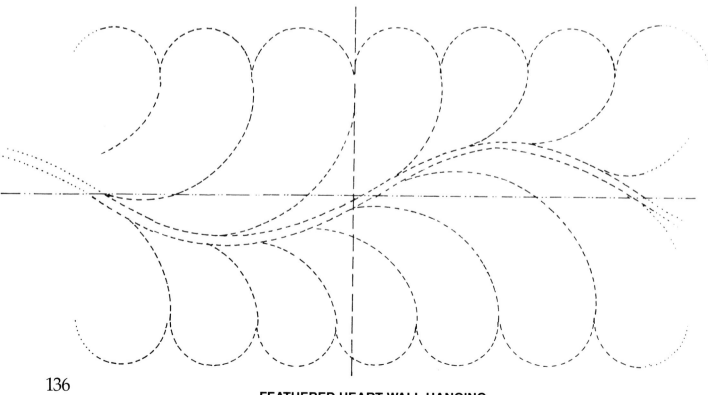

FEATHERED HEART WALL HANGING

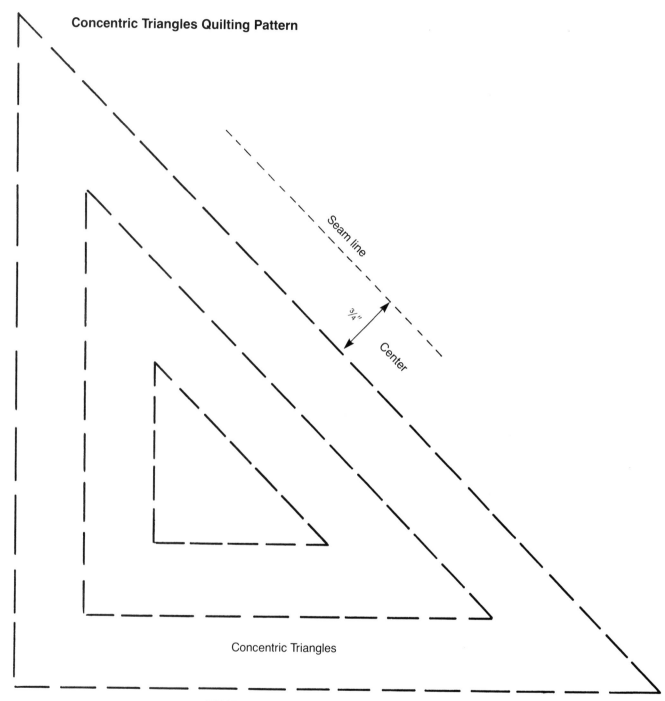

Concentric Triangles Quilting Pattern

Seam line

3/4"

Center

Concentric Triangles

FEATHERED HEART WALL HANGING

1. With a removable marker draw a 22½-inch square on the muslin. Mark the square in fourths and diagonals according to Figure B.

   Lightly mark a second square 2¾ inches inside the lines of the 22½-inch square, and a third square 5½ inches inside the original square, matching the corners with the marked diagonals. The small center square will hold the large feathered heart (Figure C). The second square will be used to align the feathered heart border pattern when marking, and the outermost square will be used as the seam line when adding the corner sections.

2. Position the center of the large feathered heart pattern where the diagonal lines cross in the 11½-inch center square and mark. The background grid will be quilted in ¾-inch increments from diagonals; mark the grid now or use your machine guide when quilting (Figure C).

3. The feathered heart border pattern is divided into two sections. The corner heart section is used to mark the border corners. One-half of the center feathered section is provided: Join the adjacent corner heart sections by tracing the center section and then reversing the pattern at mid-point to continue tracing.

Figure B

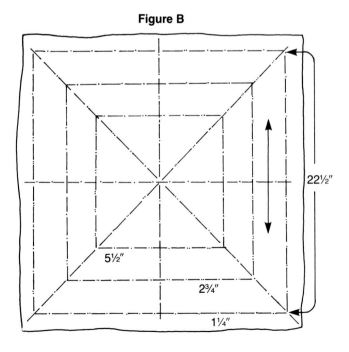

5½"
2¾"
1¼"
22½"

Figure C

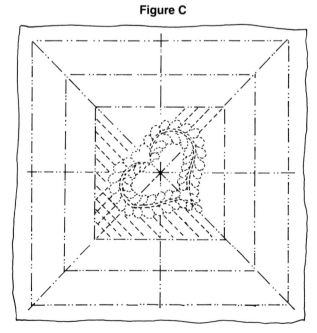

Study the marking diagram carefully (Figures D-1, D-2, D-3). Mark the corner heart sections first: Align each corner heart with a corner of the second square along line W (Figure D-1). Then draw one-half of the center feathered section by overlapping the dotted lines of the feathered and heart sections at lines X and Y (Figure D-2). Reverse the center feathered section to complete the pattern. Match each center half heart with the midpoint of the second square at line Z (Figure D-3).

Figure D-1

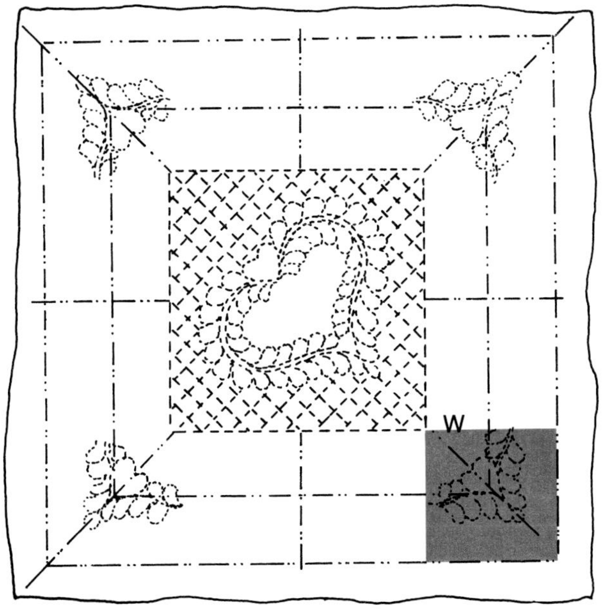

Figure D-2

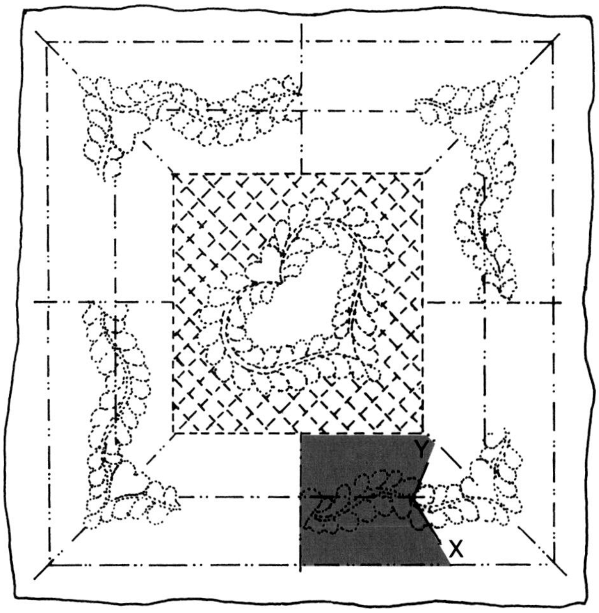

X overlap with Y

Figure D-3

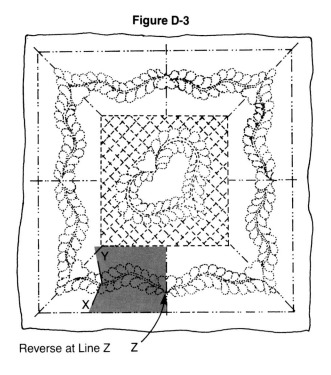

Reverse at Line Z   Z

Marking the Corner Sections

1. Mark and cut the four corner sections from the 22-inch squares as follows: Mark the diagonal across each brown fabric square; then mark a seam line 1 inch from each side of the diagonal. Cut these marked squares along with the batting and backing fabric squares in half diagonally.

2. On each corner section, find the center point of the marked seam line. Measure 11¼ inches from the center in each direction and put a dot to mark the ends of each seam line (Figure E).

Figure E

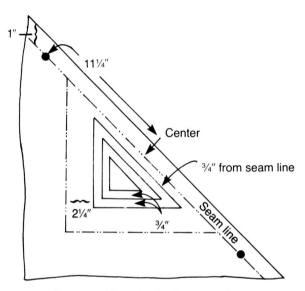

1"

11¼"

Center

¾" from seam line

Seam line

2¼"

¾"

Placement lines for feathered border

3. Mark the three concentric triangles using the pattern provided, matching the pattern center with the seam line center. The hypotenuse of the largest triangle should be ¾ inch from the seam line (Figure E).

4. Mark a horizontal placement line for the feathered border 2¼ inches outside the outermost triangle legs (Figure E). The feathered border pattern is divided into two sections. Align the border placement lines on the marked line. Mark the corner section first (Figure F). Then, on one leg, there is a partial portion of the straight section and a full straight section (Figure F). On the other leg there are two full straight sections. Overlap dotted lines as necessary to mark the border for each corner section.

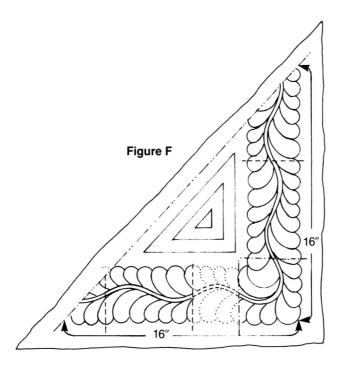

Figure F

Quilting

1. Layer each section with batting and backing. Pin or baste the layers together.
2. Here is an opportunity to try several techniques. There are no right and wrong choices, but I quilted this piece working out from the large muslin center section first. It seemed a natural for the long parallel lines in the center of the large feathered heart to be machine-guided with the built-in even-feed in place. Then I switched to free motion for the feathers. I have stressed looking for continuous-line patterns and avoiding overstitching whenever possible. Feathered designs create a unique situation where overstitching is often justified.

Feathered Quilting

With feathered designs, there are three choices:

1. Overstitch where "feathers" touch.
2. Redraw the design, separating the feathers and stitch on both sides of the newly created gap.
3. Start-and-stop-stitch on each feather, which necessitates knotting, clipping, and possibly spending time hiding thread ends in the batting.

Generally, I choose number 1 (Figure G), free-motion quilting and overstitching, especially when using invisible thread. Even though I was using the decorative rayon thread, free motion was my choice in the feathered section of the quilt.

Figure G

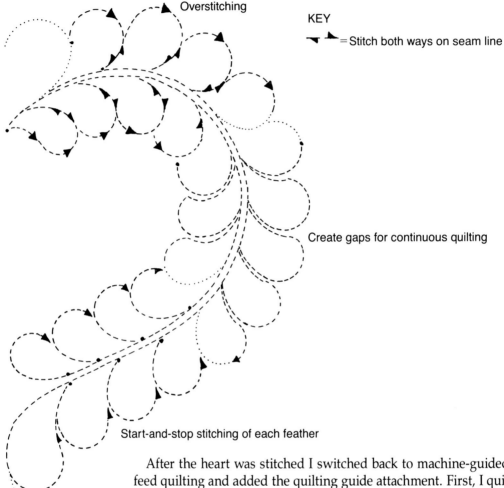

Overstitching

KEY

↙ ◤ = Stitch both ways on seam line

Create gaps for continuous quilting

Start-and-stop stitching of each feather

After the heart was stitched I switched back to machine-guided, even-feed quilting and added the quilting guide attachment. First, I quilted the diagonal positioning lines that went through the center of the square, using the guide set at ¾ inch, which eliminated marking the grid behind the heart. There were a few places where the line continued on the opposite side of the heart, so I had to stop and draw a line. If you lose track of your spacing, you will have to do the same. Stop-and-start-stitch as close to the stitched heart and the marked square as possible. In the grid it was necessary to stop-and-start on each line and deal with thread ends. (Some machines have a tie-off stitch that will adequately knot the threads on the back of the quilt.) I prefer to stop every eight or ten rows and take care of the thread ends so that I do not start stitching them into the new stitching lines.

Then I removed the machine-quilting guide and stitched the small marked square. That completed the center square. Moving on to the feathered border on the muslin section was like the feathered heart. Again, I machine-guided the center parallel lines and free-motion-quilted the feathered section, overstitching when necessary.

When I picked up the first corner, I confidently proceeded in the same way, machine-guiding center lines and free-motion, overstitching feathers. Suddenly, I didn't like the look of things. It didn't take long to realize that because I had chosen the thicker decorative thread, creating relatively high contrast between the fabric and thread, the overstitched areas jumped out at me. This was really compounded when I got to some of the feathers that have a very long common line. My decision was simple. I switched back to machine-guided and chose start-and-stop rather than overlap stitching for the feathered borders. This is not difficult. Amazingly, it didn't even seem to take a long time. In addition, I have a neatly tufted quilt back because it was also easy for me to choose to knot my threads on the back and clip them to ¼ inch. I wasn't willing to thread each loose thread end individually into a needle and hide it in the quilt batting.

Another solution would have been to switch to matching or invisible thread and overstitch, but I wanted the ecru thread. One of the wonderful things about quilting is that when it's your quilt, you can make the decisions and do what you want. An interesting footnote is that I did not remove the first section of stitching that I found so offensive when holding it 10 inches from my nose. Now when I look at the quilt and try to show someone where the offending area is, it is very difficult to find.

Assembling the Quilt Top

The corner sections are added to the quilt top in a method similar to Quilt-As-You-Sew Block Assembly Without Finishing Strips (page 116).

1. Trim the muslin center section to 23½ inches square, which includes ½-inch seam allowances. This is done most easily with a large square acrylic ruler and the rotary cutter. Trim the diagonal line of the corner pieces ½ inch from the drawn seam line.

2. Place a corner section along the center section, right sides facing. Carefully match the drawn seam lines, the ends of the seam lines, and the raw edges. Lay pieces down so that the top layer of fabric is the backing fabric of the center section. Pull that layer back and carefully pin the remaining layers together. Stitch the seam through the remaining five layers of fabric and batting. Trim away excess batting in the seam allowance.

3. Add the corner section to the opposite side of the quilt center, in the same manner. Basting seams is a rarity for me, but I would recommend basting the third and fourth corners in place to make sure that the quilting design and edges line up properly.

4. Secure the loose edges of backing for the center section. Turn under the loose backing fabric ½ inch, so that it is even with the stitching line where the two sections were joined together. Slip-stitch the folded edge in place directly on top of the seam line, using the seam line as an anchor and a guide when stitching. At the corners, clip into the seam allowance and refold the backing fabric as necessary.

Finishing the Quilt

Before adding the French-fold binding, trim the quilt top to 33½ inches square. This is done most easily with a large acrylic ruler and the rotary cutter.

A ⅜-inch French-fold binding completes the quilt. (Refer to page 198.)

8

A MACHINE QUILTER'S PICNIC

The more experienced you are with machine-quilting techniques, the more obvious it is to see the possibilities for using several of them on a quilt. You could, for example, include quilted motifs that need filler patterns to set them off along with free-motion designs that require anchoring with a few rows of machine-guided, in-the-ditch quilting.

What is less obvious is the speed and the variety achieved when machine and hand quilting are combined. For me, the most typical combination features machine in-the-ditch quilting on the long seams and Modified Quilt-As-You-Sew borders with hand quilting in the blocks. This approach cuts the amount of time required to hand-quilt without reducing the appeal.

The next project wraps up the subject of machine quilting for me because it is virtually a sampler of machine-quilting techniques. I guess it could have been named "Machine Quilting Is a Picnic." A few additional thoughts and techniques follow.

Picnic Basket Quilt

Selecting the Fabric

A selection of twenty-seven different prints is showcased in this wall hanging. The fabrics chosen for the baskets themselves reflect the many things that may be found in picnic baskets. Contrasting handles and bands, and geometric print backgrounds complete the quilt blocks. Sashing strips and borders are pieced from several prints, most notably a fabric designed as a red and white checked tablecloth, complete with ants. This fabric continues the theme, and says it all for me about picnics. Ants from this fabric were even used as fusible appliqué randomly across the quilt border.

A less complex arrangement, if you don't have this many fabrics–or don't want to shop for them–is to pick two sets of three fabrics. Make five blocks of one combination and four blocks of the other, and alternate them in the layout.

Cutting the Fabric

A typical Quilt-As-You-Sew quilt has identically sized blocks, which are the basic unit size for cutting backing and batting and for assembling the quilt top. You will see that the Picnic Basket Quilt contains some blocks with a sashing strip on the side, other blocks with a sashing strip on the bottom, still others with two sashing strips, and a single block with no sashing strips. For me, rather than bothering to keep track of all these different sizes and shapes, it was easier to cut all backing and batting 18 inches square and cut away any extra as I worked.

1. Cut nine 14½-inch squares from assorted fabrics for the basket background squares. Cut nine 18½-inch squares of backing fabric and batting.
2. Press paper-backed fusible product to the wrong side of your chosen basket fabrics. Using the pattern on page 147, cut nine Picnic Baskets from assorted fabrics.
3. Cut nine matching Basket Handles and Basket Rims to coordinate with the baskets.
4. To create the illusion of dimension, a small piece of fabric representing the inside of the basket handle is fused beside the handle. This fabric is just the wrong side of the handle fabric in all the baskets shown. Press paper-backed fusible product to the right side of these scraps for Inside Basket Handles. Cut nine Inside Basket Handles from the wrong side of handle fabric.
5. Cut twelve sashing strips from assorted fabric, 3 inches wide by 14½ inches long. Cut four 3-inch squares of assorted fabric for corner blocks. The quilt shown uses pieced fabric strips for the sashing.

Appliquéing the Baskets

Fusible appliqué was the method of choice for the quilt shown (page 144).

A small scrap of fabric was arranged as a napkin and tucked "inside" (underneath) one basket before fusing the basket into place.

Because this is a Quilt-As-You-Sew project, do not sew around the edges of the appliqué until the quilt block is layered with batting and backing.

SIZE

54¾ × 54¾ inches
Block Size: 14 inches square

MATERIALS REQUIRED

Nine 16-inch squares of assorted fabrics for blocks

Nine assorted 6- × 13-inch scraps for appliquéd baskets

Nine assorted 5- × 11-inch scraps for appliquéd bands and handles

2⅛ yards of paper-backed fusible product

½ yard of fabric for sashing (assorted scraps, if desired)

4⅛ yards of fabric for backing, including finishing strips

⅞ yard of fabric for border (assorted scraps, if desired)

3½ yards of cotton batting, or twin size packaged batting

⅝ yard of fabric for French-fold binding

Assembling the Blocks

1. Lay a backing square wrong side up and top with a batting square.
2. Layer each appliquéd block on top of batting and backing squares, carefully matching all raw edges at top left corner of blocks (Figure A).
3. Arrange the blocks in three rows of three blocks each according to your preferred layout. Label each block according to its position, Row 1, Block A; Row 1, Block B; and so on (Figure B).

Adding the Sashing

1. Study the assembly diagram carefully (Figure C). Sew a 3-inch square corner block to the end of four bottom sashing strips for Blocks 1-A, 1-B, 2-A, and 2-B.
2. Sashing strips are added stitch and flip. Sew a sashing strip to the right side of Blocks 1-A, 1-B, 2-A, 2-B, 3-A, and 3-B (Figure D). Sew a sashing strip to the bottom of Blocks 1-C and 2-C. Sashing strips with corner blocks are sewn to the bottom of Blocks 1-A, 1-B, 2-A, and 2-B. Double-check against Figure C as you sew.

Figure B

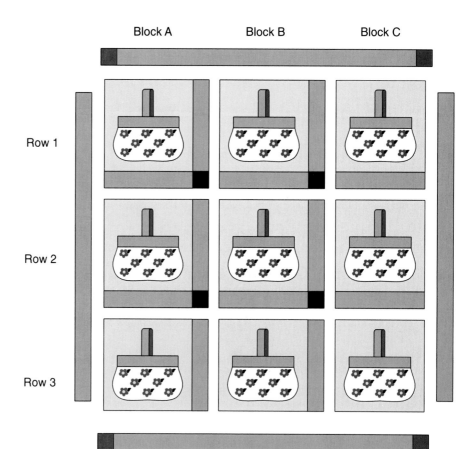

Figure C

Figure D

146

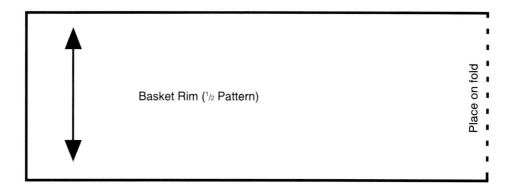

Basket Rim (½ Pattern)

Place on fold

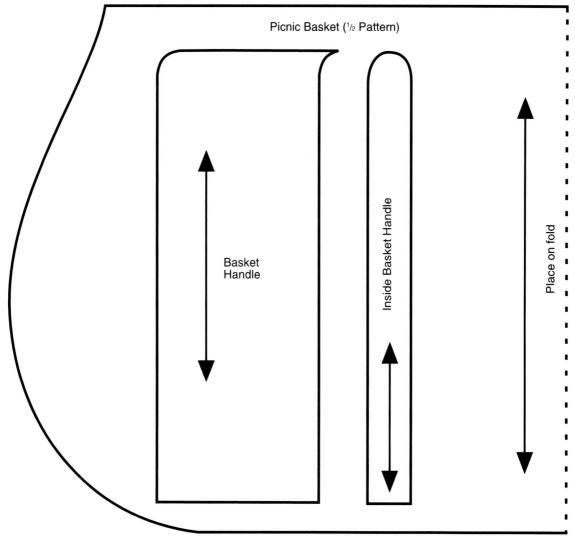

Picnic Basket (½ Pattern)

Basket
Handle

Inside Basket Handle

Place on fold

All pieces are fused; no seam allowances

Quilting the Blocks

If your baskets are fused in place, the edges can be secured with machine zigzag stitching now. This is a good place to experiment with decorative stitches on your machine, as well as with such specialty threads as metallic and variegated colors.

Machine stitching is easier and more attractive when continuous stitching is utilized. Study the design, and plan to begin stitching in a position that allows you to move through the block without starting and stopping and clipping threads.

Add any additional machine quilting now. Do not quilt into the seam allowance. Let the fabric design inspire your stitching, or use free-motion quilting (pages 106–109).

Because every basket and every background fabric is different, it seemed that it would be fun to quilt every block differently. This isn't necessary, but it made it fun for me, and the quilt really becomes a sampler of machine-quilting ideas.

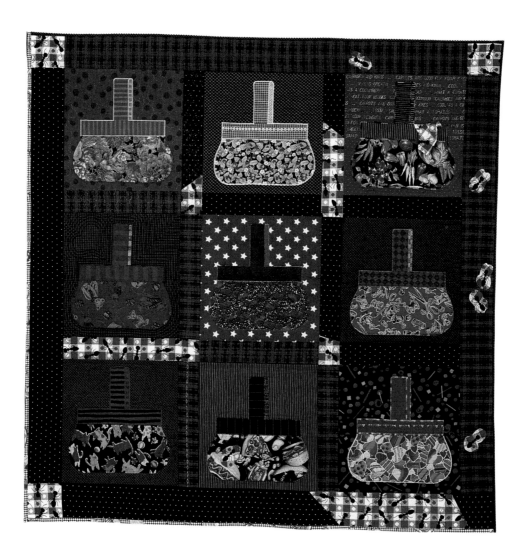

Trimming the Blocks

1. Trim the blocks to size carefully, allowing for two seam allowances. This is done most easily with a large acrylic square and a rotary cutter. Blocks 1-A, 1-B, 2-A, and 2-B are trimmed to 17 inches square. Blocks 1-C and 2-C are trimmed to 14½ inches wide by 17 inches long. Blocks 3-A and 3-B are trimmed to 17 inches wide by 14½ inches long. Block 3-C is trimmed to 14½ inches square.
2. Trim the batting an additional ¼ inch, so it will not be caught in the seam allowance when joining blocks into rows or when adding the border. The sashing fabric is quilted heavily enough that the batting will not need to be caught in the seam.

Assembling the Blocks into Rows

1. Assemble the blocks in three horizontal rows of three blocks each (Figure C).
2. Because the seams used to add the sashing strips extend to the edge of the block, separate finishing strips must be used to join the blocks into rows. See Quilt-As-You-Sew Block Assembly with Finishing Strips (Virginia Reel Quilt, page 60). Cut four finishing strips on the lengthwise grain, 1½ inches wide by 18½ inches long, and two strips 1½ inches wide by 16 inches long for Row 3.

Joining the Rows

Finishing strips are used to join the three rows of blocks to each other. (See page 61, Virginia Reel Quilt.) Cut two strips of fabric 1½ inches wide by 49 inches long. When the quilt interior is completed, it should measure 47½ inches square.

Making and Adding the Borders

1. For the quilt shown, the 3½-inch finished border was pieced from assorted scraps in the same manner as sashing strips; then it was added using the standard Quilt-As-You-Sew method (page 193).
2. Add random fusible appliqué, if desired, to the border. Complete the border with machine quilting. As with quilting the blocks, this is a good place to experiment with specialty threads and decorative stitches on your machine.

Finishing the Quilt

A separate ⅜-inch French-fold binding is used to finish the quilt. (See page 198 for details.)

Some Finishing Details   Perhaps the only consistent thing in the quilt was that, even though the baskets had many different decorative stitches, all the handles were finished with a satin stitch. I don't think I could count how many different threads I played with, but it is easy to see variety of metallic, variegated, and regular rayon decorative threads.

A few of the baskets photograph especially well, whereas some of the others have to be appreciated up close. The fabric in the basket in Block A in Row 1 (see the top left photo on page 150) was selected to represent fruit that you might take on a picnic. Some observers who have looked at the background fabric and the free-motion circular quilting have suggested

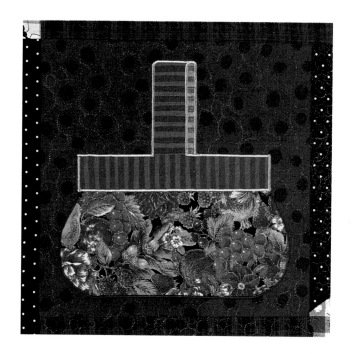

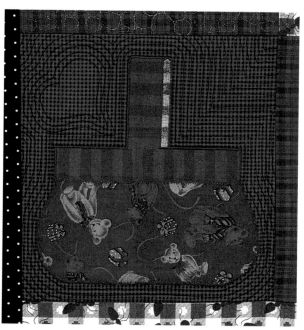

that my grapes turned into "bubbly" just in time for the picnic. Obviously, the fabric inspired where to quilt the circles.

Block A in Row 2 (see the top right photo on page 150) features echo quilting (see page 153 for a description of this technique) as a background filler and shows what happens when two motifs run together.

The random straight, but angled, lines in the background of Block A in Row 3 make an unusual and effective filler. The assorted colors used add extra interest.

Probably my favorite block is Block C in Row 1, Eat Your Veggies (see the bottom photo on page 150). I chose one of the programmed alphabets in my sewing machine and interfaced it with my computer. Modern technology made it quick and easy to quilt all of those messages into the block. You can do the same with any machine that has an alphabet, though it may take longer and require more stopping and starting.

WRAPPING UP

Quilting on Fused Quilts

The Scrappy Star Wall Hanging (page 75) has fused stars, and the Picnic Basket Quilt has fused baskets and handles. Sometimes fusing even more of the quilt makes sense. In those cases, I usually fuse the design in place first and then layer the quilt. I always secure the fused edge in some way. Sometimes I get into decorative stitches like those on the Picnic Basket Quilt.

When I want the finish to be subtle, not flashy, I zigzag the fused edges with a narrow, short zigzag stitch, invisible thread, and a small needle. Adhesive on the fused area prevents the fibers around the needle hole from closing normally, and the invisible thread doesn't begin to fill it; so the smaller the needle, the smaller the hole. The zigzag stitch is, of course, machine-guided, which means excessive turning on some projects. On some fabrics the zigzag stitch hits the fabric so consistently between the same threads that it begins to fray. Quiver quilting is a good solution to these two problems.

Using Double Needles

Just in case you glossed over the section on straight-line filler patterns and missed the pictures of fabrics quilted with double needles (page 100), I want to mention them again. A double needle gives you twice the impact for the same amount of work. Two top threads are required. They thread through the controls together, and then separate, so each needle gets its own thread. There is, of course, only one bobbin thread, which makes a zigzag-look stitch on the reverse side.

There are many fabric artists caught somewhere between surface design and quilting who are tucking, puckering, scrunching, and permanently manipulating fabric to put into their creative work. If you are leaning that way, double and triple needles would be even more of an asset.

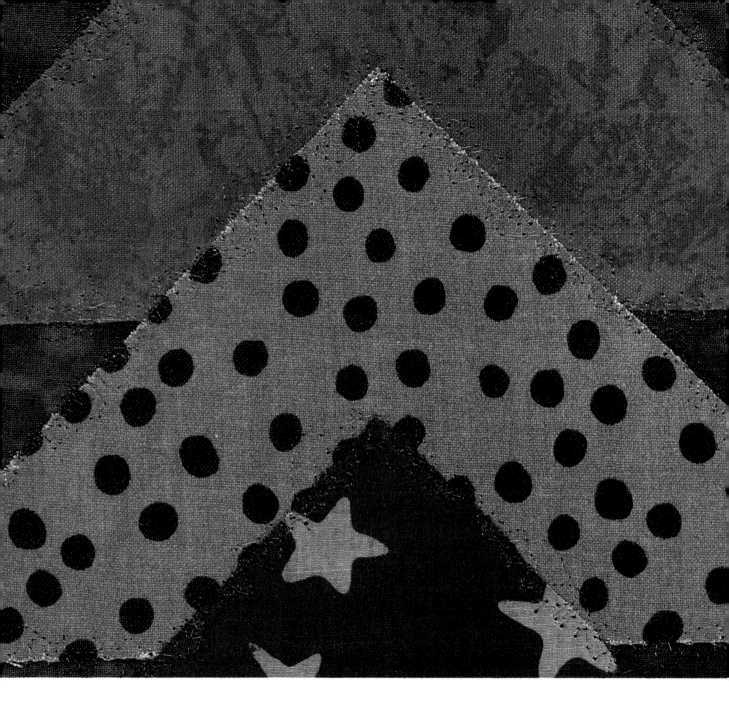

Quiver Quilting

One day when I was working on a complex fused quilt, I created *quiver quilting* (see the photo above). This is free-motion quilting with the quilter acting as a zigzag setting. Just move the quilt in tiny back-and-forth (quivering) movements, so that the edge of the fused fabric is held down with erratic zigzaglike stitches. The irregularity of the quiver prevents any forced fraying. At the same time, like any free-motion quilting, this method eliminates the constant turning of the project being quilted.

Quilting from the Back

If you fall in love with a thread that is thicker than most needle eyes, there is a good chance you can put it in the bobbin, turn the quilt upside down, and quilt from the back. The thick, decorative thread will appear on the front of the quilt, giving you the effect wanted. Sometimes the bobbin stitch is not as pretty as the top-stitch, so be sure to sample the effect before beginning.

You might also want to quilt from the back if you are having trouble marking the fabric surface. Specialty fibers, such as lamé and Ultrasuede, may not accept marks as readily as cotton, or the fabric may be dark, giving you qualms about removing the marks later. When you mark an asymmetrical design on the back of a quilt, don't forget that it will appear in reverse on the front side.

Echo Quilting

Echo quilting is really a kind of filler or background quilting. The pattern is created by stitching successive, evenly spaced lines around a motif or appliqué. You work from the center out, adding new lines until you run out of space or run into another quilting design. The look resembles the hand quilting done on traditional Hawaiian quilts. By machine, echo is easily accomplished with free-motion quilting. Best of all, there is no marking. To get a better idea of the technique, take a look at the red basket on the Picnic Basket Quilt (page 150). The entire block is filled with echo quilting and includes a quilted heart.

Trapunto

Trapunto is a technique that adds lots of surface texture to your work. The design is stitched through two layers of fabric. Narrow sections of the design are filled by running a yarn-threaded tapestry needle through the sewn channel. Larger parts of the design are slit from the back and stuffed with polyester fiberfill so they puff out. After stuffing, the slits are whipstitched shut. It is a nice touch to add some hand quilting and embellishments of ribbon and buttons.

9

A GALLERY OF MACHINE QUILTERS

Just as art galleries showcase exciting and prominent artists, this chapter is designed to spotlight and introduce a few of my favorite machine quilters, each an artist in her own right. It is my small way of paying tribute to a few of the people I think have been and are contributing greatly to machine quilting. As a bonus, several are sharing techniques in project form.

HARRIET HARGRAVE

The first artist I would like to introduce in the gallery is Harriet Hargrave. My husband and I owned a manufacturing and publishing company when I first met Harriet, who was teaching quilting and other machine arts in her Colorado store. We asked her to travel and teach for us, as well. I can still remember introducing Harriet to a class at a wholesale quilt market in 1982. "Five years ago," I said, "I wouldn't have thought of machine quilting on the surface of the quilt, but that was before I met Harriet. Don't miss her presentation." Well, a lot of curious, but doubting, shopowners thronged around Harriet at her 45-minute presentation. Afterward, one shop owner summed it up perfectly when she said to me, "An hour ago, I wouldn't have considered machine quilting, but now I will!"

Harriet's outstanding machine quilting is epitomized in her heirloom "Blue Medallion" (see photo on page 155). I didn't ask Harriet to give a tip or send a project for this book; her techniques are well documented in her own books. I dare say anyone who is doing machine quilting, especially free-motion quilting, can trace some of their methods back to Harriet. People who have not learned directly from Harriet most likely have taken a class from someone Harriet taught, have been inspired by a quilt made by someone she taught, or have learned from her books.

When I spoke to Harriet about this book and told her I wanted to acknowledge her role in inspiring machine quilters, she laughed and asked if I remembered a note I had sent her in 1983. At that time, she was writing her first book and was feeling discouraged. I sent her some words of support, and if ever I was prophetic, it was then. Here's what I said:

Harriet,

Someday quilt historians will probably write, "In the mid-1980s a small group of quilt enthusiasts began promoting quality machine quilting. The movement grew rapidly, and by the 1990s skill in manipulating a machine was considered as valuable as skill with your hands."

It might go on–"One of the earliest recognized authorities was Harriet Hargrave, a young quilter from Colorado. A sewing machine enthusiast, her early efforts were done almost apologetically as a 'substitute' for handwork. She quickly realized that the many people who love machine work and quilts deserve equal recognition with those who love hand-work. Her ideas helped many other machine sewers to express themselves."

Think positively!

Marti

All I can add is that I'm thrilled that I wrote this note. I feel honored that Harriet both kept it and sent me a copy now.

CARYL BRYER FALLERT

In 1989 machine quilters everywhere stood taller. That was the year Caryl Bryer Fallert walked away with the Best of Show award at the American Quilter's Society Show in Paducah, Kentucky, for her quilt Corona II: Solar Eclipse (below). This was clearly the most prestigious award a machine-pieced and quilted quilt had ever received. Caryl is a popular teacher and continues to make prize-winning quilts and outstanding garments, many with her famous rainbows of hand-dyed fabrics.

DSI Studios, photographer. From the collection of the Museum of the American Quilter's Society, 215 Jefferson St., Paducah, KY 42002.

DEBRA WAGNER

Since the first AQS show in 1985 there has been a hand-quilting workmanship award. In 1993, in recognition of the importance and popularity of machine quilting, an award for the Best Machine Workmanship was created. It was another landmark event for machine quilters. Debra Wagner was the recipient of the first award for her quilt, Floral Urns (below). Debra has won many prizes and done much to contribute to the stature of machine quilting today.

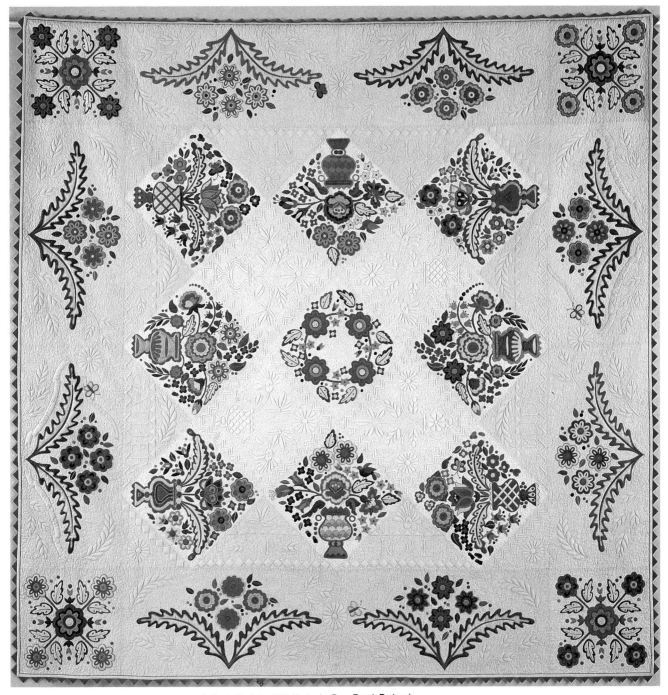

DSI Studios, photographer. From the American Quilter's Society, 5801 Kentucky Dam Road, Paducah, KY 42002.

LIBBY LEHMAN'S RIBBON STITCHING

Libby Lehman of Houston, Texas, is a very talented, award-winning studio quilt artist and teacher. She is well known for her exciting use of color and inventive machine quilting. You can see the dramatic effect of her ribbon-stitching technique on her Ribbon Quartet Quilt below. The pillow project she designed for this book shares the ribbon technique but is not actually quilted. (You may do additional quilting if desired.)

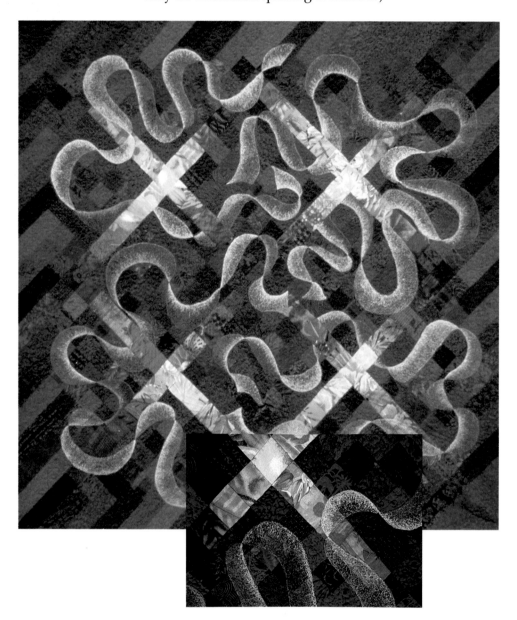

TIP: Set the Machine for Ribbon Stitching

Load the bobbin with fine polyester thread and the machine with gold metallic thread. Lower the tension slightly. With the darning foot and top-stitch needle on the machine, lower the feed dogs.

All Wrapped Up Pillow

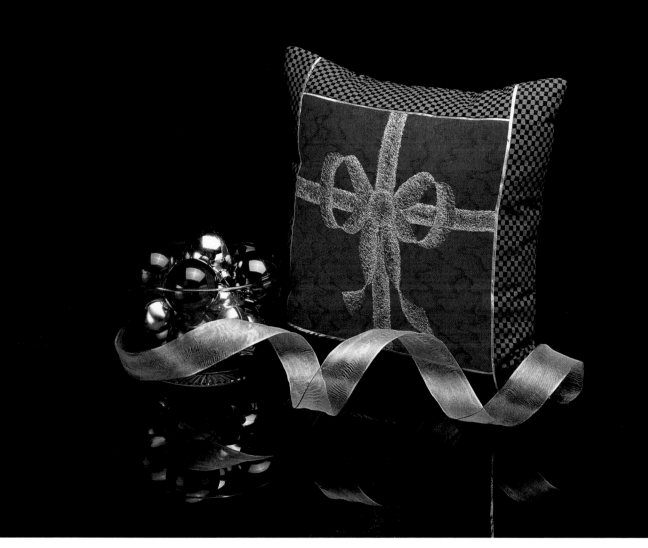

Marking the Design

1. Enlarge the ribbon design (Figure A) to make bow 7 inches across and trace onto freezer paper or stabilizer, such as Totally Stable by Sulky®. To transfer the design without having to mark the fabric, center the paper (waxed side down) or stabilizer (adhesive side down) on the right side of the pillow top and press with a warm iron.
2. Set up the machine for ribbon stitching.
3. Stitch through the design to transfer it from the freezer paper or stabilizer to the fabric. Tear away the paper or stabilizer. Both products can be removed easily without leaving a residue.

SIZE
14 x 14 inches

MATERIALS REQUIRED
14-inch square of red fabric for pillow top

14-inch square of freezer paper or iron-on tear-away stabilizer

¼ yard of green fabric for border, cut crosswise and pieced

⅛ yard of gold lamé fabric for border, cut crosswise and pieced

15-inch square of green fabric for backing

14-inch square pillow form

Gold metallic thread

Variegated yellow rayon thread

Darning foot to fit your sewing machine

10-inch screw-type embroidery hoop

Figure A

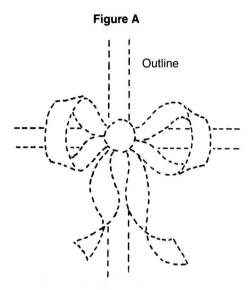

Outline

Ribbon Stitching the Pillow Top

1. Place the pillow top fabric in the embroidery hoop, and tighten the fabric as much as possible.
2. Reduce the upper thread tension. Check the bobbin tension (page 25). Draw the bobbin thread up to the top. Take a few small straight stitches to anchor the threads, and clip the thread ends. Now set the machine on zigzag.
3. Start filling in the ribbon area with gold metallic stitching (Figure B), making it as open or dense as you wish. Rotate the hoop randomly so that the stitches go in all directions. The stitches should sit on the surface, rather than pucker the fabric (Figure C). Stop and reposition the hoop as often as necessary to fill in all of the ribbon areas.

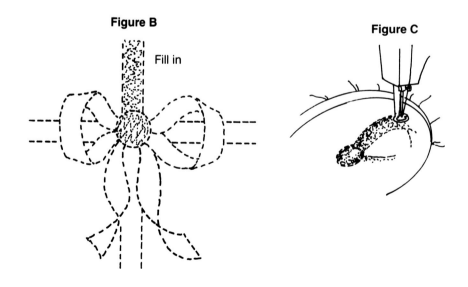

Figure B

Fill in

Figure C

4. Load the machine with variegated rayon thread. Ribbon stitch along each edge of the ribbon and one edge of each bow section to create shading (Figure D-1). Lighter sections of the thread should be concentrated along the opposite edge (Figure D-2).

5. Remove the completed pillow top from the hoop and press from the back side, using a press cloth.

6. Trim the pillow top to 11 inches square, which includes ¼-inch seam allowances. This is done most easily with a large square acrylic ruler and the rotary cutter.

Figure D-1

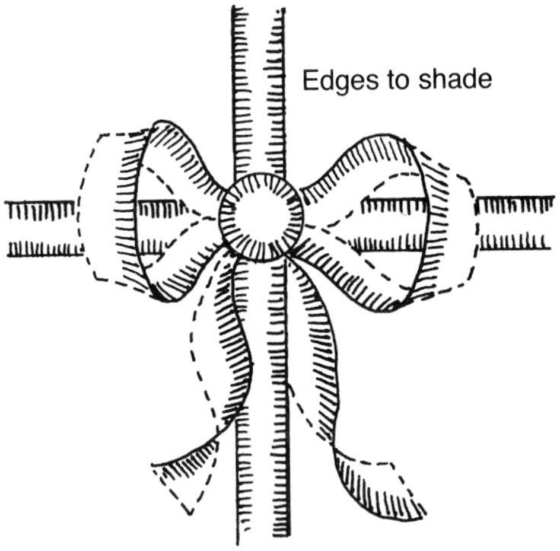

Edges to shade

Figure D-2

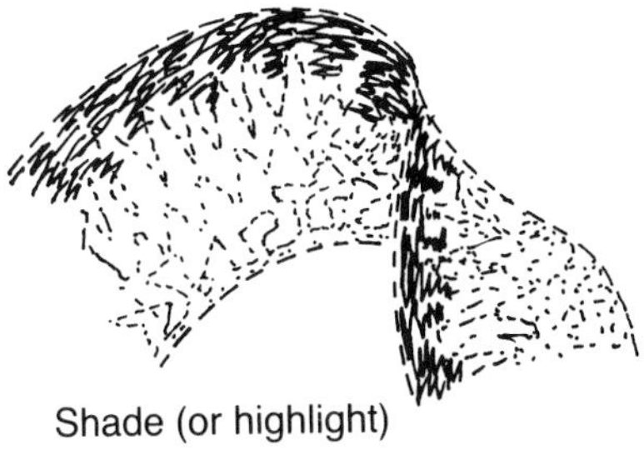

Shade (or highlight)

Making and Adding the Borders

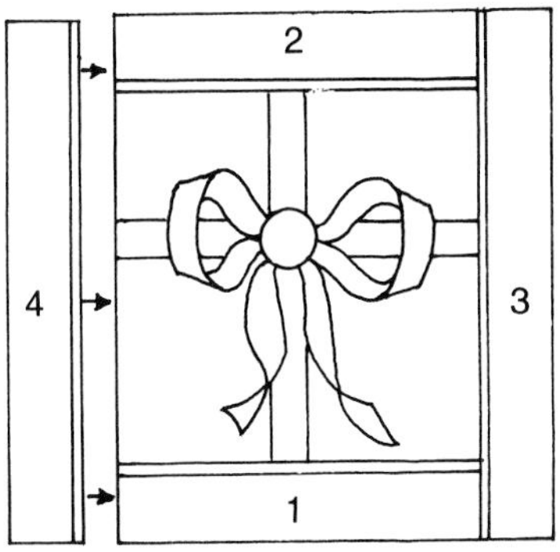

1. Cut 2-inch-wide border strips from green fabric, two 11 inches long and two 14½ inches long. Cut ¾-inch-wide border strips from gold lamé fabric, the same lengths as the green strips.

2. Matching lengths, and with right sides facing, sew the gold and green border strips together. Press the seam allowance toward the green strip.

3. Sew the 11-inch border strips along the top and bottom edges of the pillow, matching raw edges of the gold border and the pillow top. Press the seam allowances toward the borders.

4. Sew the remaining border strips to the pillow sides, again matching raw edges of the gold border and the pillow top (Figure E). Press the seam allowances toward the borders.

Figure E

161

The completed pillow top should measure 14½ inches square, including ¼-inch seam allowances.

Finishing the Pillow

1. Place pillow top and bottom right sides facing. Sew all around the outside edge, leaving an opening along the bottom for turning. Clip the corners of the seam allowance diagonally.

2. Turn the pillow right side out. Insert the pillow form through the opening, and slip-stitch closed.

HARI WALNER'S FREE-MOTION CONTINUOUS LINES

Hari Walner came to quilting from a career in illustration and graphic arts. She has been creating beautiful continuous-line quilting designs since 1988 and markets them through her company, Beautiful Publications (see Resource List, page 202). Her friendly, humorous encouragement to beginning machine quilters is legendary. The table scarf project she shares gives you many opportunities to practice free-motion continuous-line quilting.

Overcoming the Fear of Free-Motion Quilting
Hari Walner

Check your insurance policies. Many policies cover damages caused by sewing machines biting or booing their operators.

Warning: Some policies do not cover psychiatric care for quilters who insist on letting their machines take advantage of them.

Tip: Read *Women Who Love Their Sewing Machines Too Much to Adjust the Tension*.

Begin with small projects and learn basic skills before tackling large items. Make bath mats, pot holders, placemats, etc.

For practice, use the fabric in your stash that you are embarrassed to admit you ever bought. You will sew more relaxed because you won't worry about ruining it. You will use it up, and then you can go out and buy more fabric.

It is possible to quilt on many older and less expensive machines. Even though we all want a high-end sewing machine (one of each, please), many of us cannot afford one. When our dream machine comes true, we will really be ready to make beautiful music.

Many people learn to play the piano before they get a Steinway.

There is much hand/eye/mind coordination involved in free-motion quilting, so allow time and practice for this communication to develop. Practice the same patience with yourself that you do when you are teaching others.

We cannot make ourselves perform a skill well, but we can let ourselves do it. (This is the **Zen** of free-motion quilting.)

Most important of all, machine quilting is fun. Have a good time.

Floral Chain Table Scarf

Cutting the Fabric

1. From muslin, cut two 8-inch squares. Also cut one 9¾-inch square, and cut on both diagonals to make four triangles (Figure A).
2. From blue print fabric, cut one 8-inch square. Also cut two 9¾-inch squares, then cut on both diagonals to make a total of eight triangles (Figure A).
3. From floral print fabric, cut six strips 1 inch wide by 8 inches long, and six strips 1 inch wide by 8½ inches long. Also cut four strips 1 inch wide by 12½ inches long, and two strips 1 inch wide by 38½ inches long.

Figure A

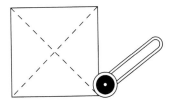

SIZE
43 x 18 inches
Block Size: 12 inches square

MATERIALS REQUIRED
½ yard of muslin
½ yard of blue tone-on-tone print fabric, including border
½ yard of floral print fabric for strips and French-fold binding
⅝ yard of backing fabric
⅝ yard of batting
Water-erasable marking pen

163

Floral Chain

Begin stitching here ↓

Floral Chain Quilting Diagram

Floral Chain Corner Motif

Making the Blocks

1. Sew 1-inch by 8-inch strips to two opposite sides of each 8-inch center square. Sew 1-inch by 8½-inch strips to the remaining opposite sides of the 8-inch squares (Figure B).

2. Sew the blue triangles to the muslin squares, and the muslin triangles to the blue square (Figure C). Sew triangles to opposite sides first.

Finished blocks should measure 12½ inches square, including ¼-inch seam allowances.

Figure B

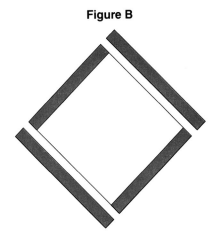

Figure C

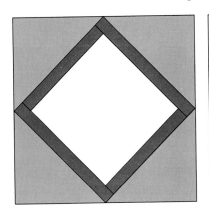
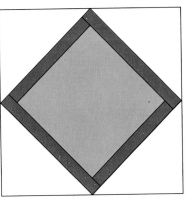

Assembling the Table Scarf

Sew a 12½-inch floral strip to each side of the middle (blue center) block. Sew a muslin center block on each side into a row (Figure D). Sew the remaining 12½-inch floral strips to each end of the row. Sew the 38½-inch floral strips to the top and the bottom of the row. The completed scarf should measure 38½ by 13½ inches, including ¼-inch seam allowances.

Figure D

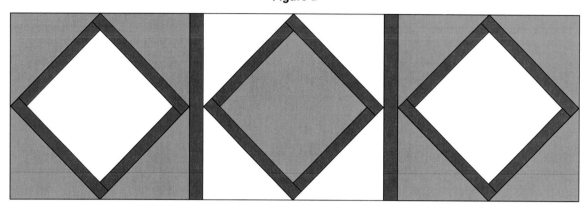

Adding the Border

The 2-inch finished-width blue print border is added the Good Old-fashioned Way (pages 192–193).

Marking the Quilting Design

Use a water-erasable marking pen to mark the quilt design. [See Chapter 6 for details on technique (pages 96–98).] Trace the complete pattern as provided on the muslin squares and corner triangles only. Refer to Figure E. The chain by itself is marked and quilted on the blue square and corner triangles.

Figure E

Adding Batting and Backing

Cut batting and backing about 2 inches bigger in all directions than the table scarf (approximately 46½ inches by 21½ inches). Place the backing wrong side up. Layer on the batting, then the table scarf top, right side up, over the batting. Use pins to hold the three layers in place.

Quilting

1. Stitch in the ditch around center squares, triangles, strips, and the border.
2. Begin stitching the center square medallion as indicated in the quilting diagram (Figure F), starting with the leaf line to bring you to the inner chain. As you make the first round from corner to corner you are quilting only one-half of that inner chain. Stitch all of each corner motif in turn, except for the second line of the leaf that you first stitched. Now stitch around the other half of the inner chain to complete the chain. Then travel back toward the outer chain via the top line of the first leaf. Finally, complete the outer chain by stitching around both lines.
3. For the corner motif, begin stitching from the center of the bottom chain. Stitch the floral motif first. Return to the chain and stitch both curved lines around the chain to complete the triangle.

Finishing the Table Scarf

Quilt border ¼ inch in from edges. Complete piece with a ⅜-inch French-fold binding of floral print (see page 198).

SHERRY SUNDAY'S PERFECTLY PAINLESS APPLIQUÉ

Sherry Sunday is a prolific award-winning quilt artist and teacher from the New Kingston, Pennsylvania, area. She is well known for her combination appliqué and patchwork machine-quilted works. When she isn't quilting, you might find her racing sports cars or scuba diving.

Sherry Sunday's perfectly painless method of appliqué utilizes freezer paper and a fabric glue stick. Sherry says Ann Oliver showed her how to use freezer paper on the wrong side of the fabric. She rushed home excited to try it and by mistake put the paper and fabric together the wrong way. For her it turned out to be a happy accident.

In Sherry's method, finished-size freezer paper templates are ironed to the right side of the appliqué fabric. Fabric glue is applied to the seam allowance on the wrong side of the appliqué, and the seam allowances are pressed under. The freezer paper is removed, and a blind stitch with invisible nylon thread is used to sew the appliqué in place. You'll get to try Sherry's technique in the following beautiful project that she designed.

Selecting the Fabric

The red metallic floral fabric is especially dramatic against the plain muslin center block and border. Reds and greens from the metallic floral are repeated in the assorted appliqué fabrics.

Cutting the Fabric

1. From muslin background fabric, cut a 19-inch square for the center block. The finished size is 18 inches; the block will be trimmed to 18½ inches before adding the corner triangles.
2. From red print fabric, cut two 13⅝-inch squares, and cut each square in half diagonally to make the four corner triangles.

Border strips will be cut and appliquéd after the quilt interior is completed.

Tracing the Pattern

The floral appliqué pattern provided is for one-fourth of the whole block. Mark the complete pattern on paper, then trace the pattern onto the fabric block with a water-erasable marking pen. (Please refer to Tracing the Pattern on page 111 for full instructions.)

Marking and Cutting the Bias Strips for the Vine Appliqué

1. Cut the 18-inch square of green fabric for the vine appliqué in half diagonally. With right sides facing, sew the straight edges together to create a parallelogram (Figure A).
2. Using the formula of four times the finished width plus ⅛ inch for fold allowance, mark the first two rows of bias strips 1⅛ inches wide (Figure B). Draw the lines parallel to the diagonal edge. Mark the entire piece of fabric into rows.

SIZE
36¾ x 36¾ inches
Block Size: 18 inches square

MATERIALS REQUIRED
1⅜ yards of muslin for center block and borders
⅜ yard each of three different red fabrics for floral appliqués
⅜ yard each of two different green fabrics for leaf appliqués
18-inch square of green fabric for bias strip vine appliqués
1⅛ yards of red metallic floral fabric for corner triangles and French-fold binding
1⅛ yards of fabric for backing
1⅛ yards of batting
Water-erasable marking pen
Freezer paper
Fabric glue stick
Wooden skewer
Invisible nylon thread
Sewing machine with blind stitch capability

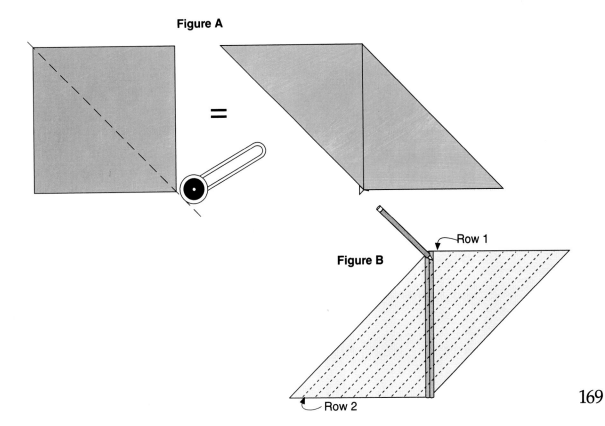

Figure A

Figure B

Row 1

Row 2

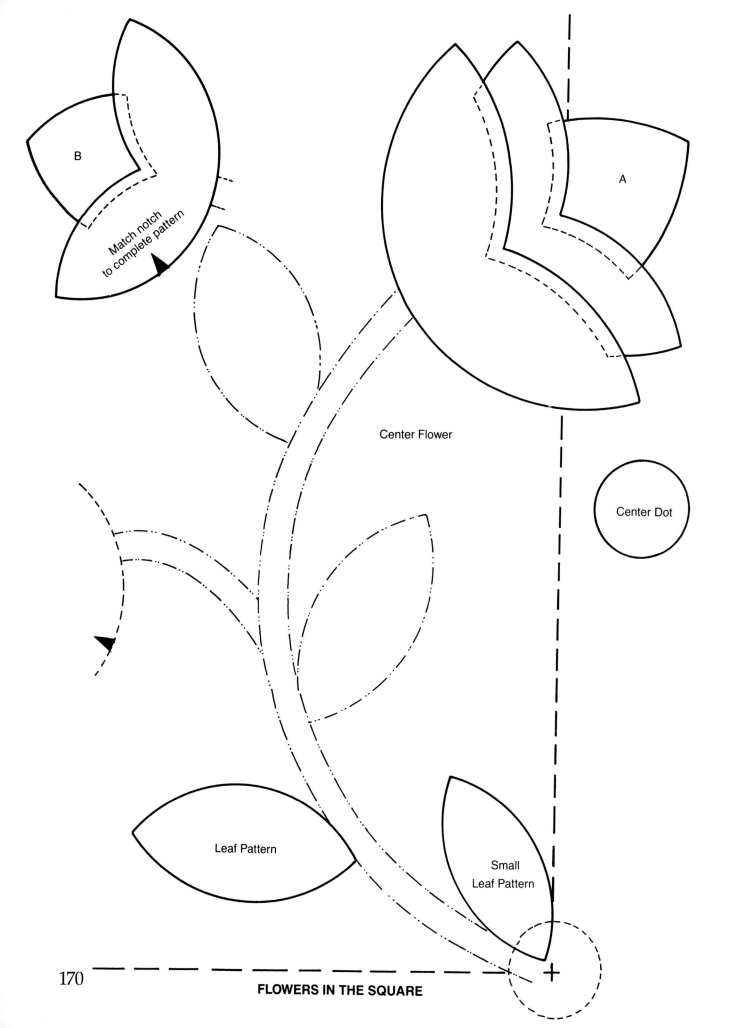

B

Match notch
to complete pattern

A

Center Flower

Center Dot

Leaf Pattern

Small
Leaf Pattern

170

FLOWERS IN THE SQUARE

FLOWERS IN THE SQUARE BORDER, CORNER

171

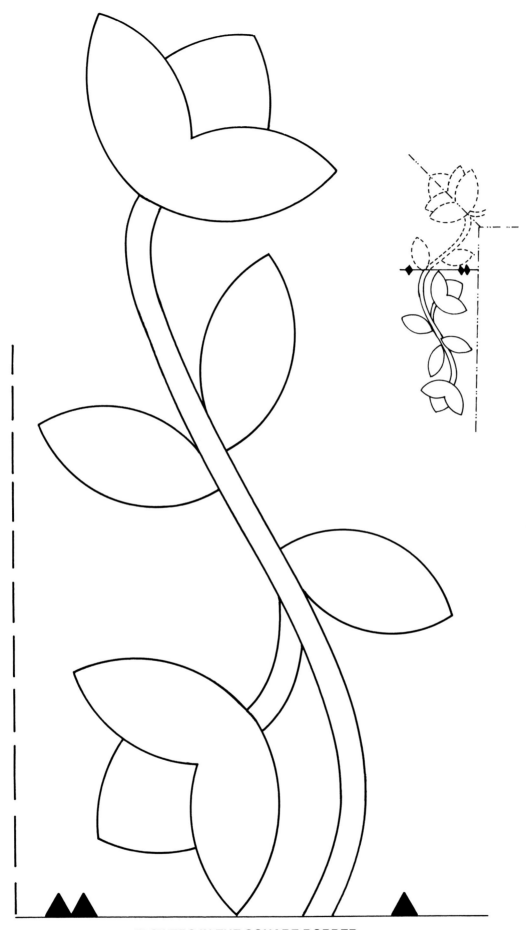

FLOWERS IN THE SQUARE BORDER

3. Lift the bottom edge and, with the right sides facing, line up the end of the second marked line on that edge with the first marked line on the top. Pin the edges carefully in place. Sew the pinned edges together.

4. With scissors, cut on the line from the end of the first offset and cut in a spiral through the entire piece (Figure C), creating one long spiral of approximately 400 inches of bias strip.

Figure C

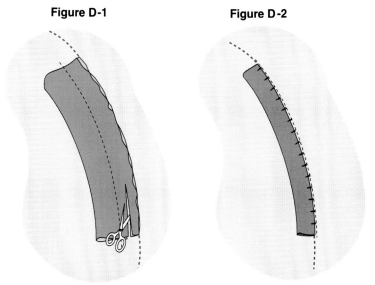

Applying the Vine Appliqué

1. Use a tape measure to determine the length to cut the bias strip for each vine. Allow a few inches extra per piece.

2. Fold the strips in half, wrong sides facing, and press. Open the strips, apply a few spots of glue, and refold.

3. Apply a fine bead of glue to the center of the stem placement line on the background fabric.

4. Place the raw edges of the folded strip along the inside of the convex (outside) curve placement line (Figure D-1). Sew a hand or machine running stitch along the center of the strip. Trim the raw edges of the strip to approximately ⅛ inch.

5. Apply a fine bead of fabric glue to the line just inside the convex edge of the placement line on the background fabric.

6. Flip the strip over, folded edge on the placement line, easing around the curves. Finger-press to catch glue. Machine blind-stitch in place with invisible thread (Figure D-2).

Figure D-1   **Figure D-2**

Blind-Stitch Appliqué

Machine appliqué is two to two and one-half times faster than hand appliqué. A blind hemstitch (or buttonhole stitch) is usually recommended for machine appliqué. The blind hemstitch creates a light V shape where the needle catches the edge of the appliqué. The buttonhole stitch does not create a V, but makes a straight stitch over and back. You will probably need to get out your machine's instruction book and experiment a little.

Setting Up the Machine for Blind-Stitch Appliqué

1. Install a fine machine needle, such as a $70/10$ or $80/11$, and an open-toe appliqué foot on the machine.
2. Use 60-weight machine embroidery thread in the bobbin. Match it to the background fabric.
3. Thread the machine with monofilament invisible nylon thread.
4. Select the blind hemstitch or buttonhole stitch on the machine. Move the needle position to the right, if possible. Reduce stitch width to halfway between 0 and 1. Reduce the stitch length to halfway between 0 and 1. Loosen the top thread tension.
5. Practice stitching. As you practice, it may be necessary to adjust stitch width and length, as well as upper thread and bobbin tensions. (Please refer to pages 24–25.)

1. Place the appliqué to the left side of the needle. Place the straight stitching line on the background fabric. Never straight-stitch on the appliqué; the appliqué will be caught by the alternate stitches (Figure D-2).
2. Sew a few stitches on the machine. Inspect and adjust if necessary. The bobbin thread should not show through the stitches on the top. Refer to the stitching diagram to secure points, edges, and curves properly (Figure E).

Figure E

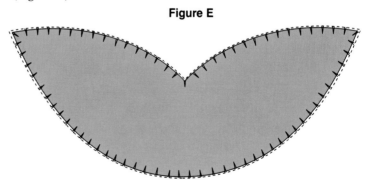

Preparing and Appliquéing the Flowers and Leaves

1. Place freezer paper over the right side of the pattern, waxed side down, and trace the exact finished size of the pattern. Although you will cut multiple freezer paper templates as needed for the total number of a particular shape, begin by cutting one template of each shape needed.

2. Rough-cut freezer paper to the size for the total number of templates needed of a particular shape. Layer four rough-cut templates together with the finished-size template on top, and fuse lightly in place at the corners with a hot, dry iron. Cut the stack of templates as one.

Cut the total number of each template needed in this manner.

3. Place the freezer paper templates, waxed side down, on the right side of the appliqué fabric. Allow ½ inch of cutting space around each template. Press with a hot, dry iron.

4. Cut out the appliqués, allowing a fat ⅛-inch to ³⁄₁₆-inch seam allowance. Cut a smooth edge, clipping concave (inside) curves and points only when necessary.

5. Use a glue stick to apply a fine bead of glue to the wrong side of the appliqué seam allowance.

6. Beginning at a straight or slightly curved area, roll the seam allowance in tiny increments and press. Use an extra spot of glue to hold any stray threads in place.

7. To turn sharp points, glue and crimp the seam to the point. The folded seam allowance may need to be trimmed. Fold the pointed tip in toward the appliqué squarely. Apply another spot of glue and fold the remaining seam allowance under.

8. Check for any unevenness from the right side, using a wooden skewer to ease seam allowances as necessary.

Prepare all appliqués in this manner. Leave the freezer paper in place until you are ready to appliqué to keep the piece clean and free of wrinkles.

9. Machine blind-stitch in place with invisible thread. The red center of the center flower is lightly stuffed with fiberfill before the appliqué is completed.

Making Dimensional Flowers Sherry has substituted Prairie Points for the appliquéd tip of the flowers shown in the pattern.

1. Cut 4½-inch squares of fabric for the larger flowers and 3-inch squares for the smaller ones.
2. Fold each square in half diagonally (Figure F).
3. Fold each side down to meet at the lower corner of the square. Trim the raw edges to remove excess fabric (Figure G).
4. Insert a prairie point into the upper edge of a flower before completing the appliqué. Do not stitch folded eges down.

Adding the Corner Triangles

Sew the red print corner triangles to the center square. The completed quilt interior should measure 26 by 26 inches, including ¼-inch seam allowances.

Adding the Border

1. The border for this quilt is 5 inches finished, cut from muslin background fabric. Cut two border strips 5½ inches wide by 26 inches long, and two strips 5½ inches wide by 36 inches long.
2. Trace the appliqué pattern onto the border strips. Appliqué the vine, flowers, and leaves into place along the border according to the directions above. The final corner appliqué will be completed after the borders are sewn to the quilt top.

Figure F

Figure G

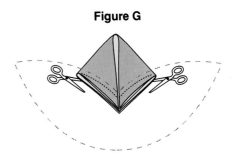

3. The appliquéd borders are added by the Good Old-fashioned Way. (Refer to pages 192–193 for details.)

4. Complete the corner appliqué.

Layering with Batting and Backing

Layer the quilt top with batting and backing.

Quilting

Quilt as desired. The photographed quilt's border is echo-quilted (see page 153) by machine around the border appliqué. The center block is free-motion quilted. The corner triangles are quilted in a grid pattern. (For a discussion of channels and grids see page 99.)

Finishing the Quilt

A ⅝-inch French-fold binding completes the quilt. (Refer to page 198 for details.)

IRIS LEE'S MACHINE CRAZY QUILTING

Even though I absolutely love crazy quilts, the idea of crazy quilting on the sewing machine never crossed my mind until I met Iris Lee. You can see why because she made all of the wonderful projects in this section. If you have a top-of-the-line machine, it is loaded with decorative stitches that you may think you will never use. Even most new moderately priced machines have a good selection of stitches. Iris selects the stitches that most resemble hand embroidery for her machine crazy quilting. Check your sewing machine manual for tips on machine settings for your decorative stitches. Then sew a sampler of all of them using shiny rayon embroidery thread. Your sampler will be a much prettier reference than the drawings.

Iris loves thread and has lots of fun selecting, changing, and combining threads to add more interest to her projects. She often finishes off her projects with embellishments and just enough hand embroidery to give the illusion that all the work is done by hand. (As you can understand, it would be impossible to give complete directions for all these projects.)

Crazy quilting is highly individual and requires the development of a personal style. The techniques are slightly different for woven and unwoven fabrics, but once you understand the basics, you should have no trouble creating projects such as those shown here. If you are planning much hand work, the lightweight Facile™ is easier to needle than Ultrasuede. Study the pictures, determine what you like most, and go for it.

MATERIALS REQUIRED

Ultrasuede, Facile, or other nonwoven fabric
 scraps
Muslin base fabric
Fabric glue stick
Assorted rayon embroidery thread and
 metallic threads
Assorted trims and embellishments

These directions reflect how to make any of these projects, not just a specific one.

Preparing the Base Material

1. Whether it's a vest or an ornament, draw the finished shape of the item onto a piece of prewashed muslin. Leave room around the shape for seam allowances plus at least an inch all around for holding. Do not cut the shape out yet.
2. Make a patchwork design inside the outline by drawing interesting straight-edged geometric shapes. Vary the sizes, but don't make them too small.
3. When satisfied with the patchwork design, mark each shape with the color to be used. Make sure no two pieces of the same color are touching.
4. Transfer the drawing to paper, and cut apart the individual patchwork pieces. Use these as patterns to cut corresponding colors of nonwoven fabric scraps.

Assembling the Patchwork

Assemble the patchwork pieces on the muslin background fabric. Use just enough glue stick on the corners of each piece to hold it in place. Let the glue dry thoroughly before continuing.

Quilting the Patchwork

1. Thread your machine. Experiment with using two threads together, which makes decorative stitches show up better. Use two spools on the top, threading the machine as if they were a single thread. Avoid breakage by not mixing rayons and metallics together.

   Schmetz needles in sizes 80–110 have a larger eye than the typical needle and are useful with multiple threads, metallics, and heavier threads. A size 100 top stitching needle works well with Facile. The size of the needle you use depends upon the kind of fabric and the size of thread you are using. (Refer to page 29.)
2. Using the decorative stitches on your sewing machine, stitch where the edges of the patchwork butt together. It will probably be necessary to loosen the needle thread tension. Be sure that the bobbin thread is not showing on top of the fabric; it is better for the decorative thread to show slightly on the underside. Experiment with your stitches, making some longer or wider than normal.

   If the center of the presser foot is positioned exactly where the two pieces of patchwork butt, the stitches extend onto each piece of patchwork. This also keeps the muslin from showing through between the pieces.

Embellishing the Patchwork

After finishing all of the decorative machine stitching, add buttons, jewels, or small charms to the piece, if desired. You may want to experiment with hand embroidery stitches inside some of the shapes, using silk buttonhole twist or embroidery thread.

Basic Crazy Quilting: Woven Fabrics

When using woven fabrics, the finished shape or pattern is cut from the fabric after all crazy quilting is completed.

Preparing the Fabric

1. Rough-cut a piece of pre-washed muslin two to three inches larger all around than the needed finished shape of the item. The patchwork pieces will be sewn to this base material. Do not cut the shape out yet.
2. Cut straight-edged geometric patchwork pieces from assorted fabric scraps. Vary the sizes, but don't make them too small.

Assembling the Patchwork

1. Begin working from the center of the large muslin base fabric outward. Place a piece of patchwork right side up on the muslin. Then place another patchwork piece on top of the first, having right sides together and one pair of raw edges aligned. Sew along the aligned edges (Figure A). It is very important for the stitching line to be straight so that the finished patchwork will lie flat.
2. Open out the patchwork piece just sewn and press it flat (Figure B).
3. Place the next piece face down along one raw edge and stitch again (Figure C). Continue stitching and flipping in a counterclockwise manner to fill the muslin base with patchwork. Vary the size and shape of the patchwork pieces used, letting the piecing determine itself. Irregularities may be trimmed away after stitching.

Most of Iris's work is stitch and flip string piecing. However, since all edges will be subsequently stitched, she does admit to turning under raw edges and using pins to hold them in place when the design dictates.

Quilting and Embellishing the Patchwork

Quilt and embellish as desired, following the directions for quilting the nonwoven fabric.

There are many wonderful machine-quilters. Pay special attention to any demonstrations at the next quilt show you attend. Try it yourself!

THE LIST GOES ON

The list of wonderful machine-quilt artists goes on and on, but we must stop. That is no reason for the inspiration of other quilters to end. Look more closely at the next quilt show you attend. You may discover that many of the quilts you thought were finished by hand were, in fact, machine quilted. You will probably see new and inventive techniques. Absorb as much as you can, incorporate the things you read and see into your own methods, but most of all, I hope that you will enjoy machine quilting!

MATERIALS REQUIRED

Silks, metallics, or other woven fabric scraps
Muslin base fabric
Fabric glue stick
Assorted rayon embroidery and metallic threads
Assorted trims and embellishments

Figure A

Figure B

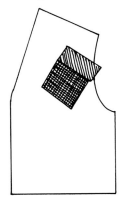

Figure C

10

WHOLE-QUILT MACHINE QUILTING

This chapter may provide all the information you expected about machine quilting. It is a very typical method for people to use for all their machine quilting. Whether you are quilting a small quilt or a large one, this information is appropriate. The quilt in the pictures on the following pages is printed patchwork fabric, perfect for practicing machine quilting. It is a full-sized queen/double bed quilt. Whatever your project, the instructions in this chapter start when you have a quilt top ready to layer and machine-quilt.

PREPARING TO QUILT

Backing

Traditionally, quilt backings have been made from a single fabric with minimal or no piecing. The most common pieced back shows a single seam running down the vertical center. But who wants to be common? I find more and more of my backings have some degree of patchwork. (It lets me use up my fabric reserves so I can justify buying more!) Unlike hand quilting, the sewing machine stitches through the extra seams with little difficulty.

If you like the look of a seamless quilt backing, you'll be interested in the 60-inch-, 90-inch-, and even 108-inch-wide fabrics being made today just for quilters. For years we have been told not to use sheets because they are too hard to needle. Recently, however, I have heard people suggesting that the 100% cotton sheets available now are worth considering.

No matter what type of backing you choose, measure your quilt top accurately. The backing should be at least 2 inches larger in all directions than the top.

Batting

Your quilt will be smoother and easier to quilt if the batting does not have bumps. If you have a good source of roll batting, buy it as close as possible to the day you intend to use it, roll or fold it as little as possible to get it home, and spread it out immediately upon arriving home.

Most quilts are filled with packaged batting, which tends to display ridges, bumps, and humps when it is unrolled. In my experience, the time spent steaming packaged batting is well spent.

1. On your ironing board or other padded surface, spread out the batting in a single layer, and lay a piece of lightweight cotton fabric over it.

2. Graze the surface of the fabric with your steam iron (see the photo below). Don't set the iron down; just run it back and forth, allowing the steam to penetrate the batting and relax the creases.
3. Lift the cloth to check your progress. When the batting underneath is smooth, reposition it and proceed to the next section in the same way.

Always double-check the size of the batting at this point. Like the backing, it should be at least 2 inches larger all around than the quilt top.

TIP: How to Piece Batting

If you must piece batting, overlap the pieces and make a new cut through both pieces at once (Diagram 1) for edges that align perfectly. Remove the excess ends. Use long, loose hand stitches to hold the butted edges together (Diagram 2).

Diagram 1

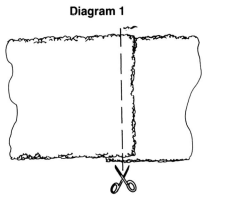

Diagram 2

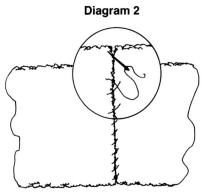

Layering

If your quilt is full-sized, try to entice a friend to help you layer it. Two of you can layer a quilt for each of you faster than either of you can layer a quilt alone. Start with a freshly pressed quilt top, backing, and a prepared (flat) batting. I like to layer on a long, narrow table similar to a folding lunchroom table. Measure and mark the center of both ends of the table with tape before you begin.

1. Fold the backing in half lengthwise, then crosswise (into quarters), wrong side in. Mark the center of each edge at the foldlines. Do the same for the batting and the quilt top, except fold the quilt top right side in.

2. Lay the folded backing fabric on the table right side up and unfold once. Align the lengthwise fold along the tape markings (see the photo below on the left), and pull the fabric smooth. (Some people like to clamp the fabric to the table, but I am perfectly happy without clamps.) Without shifting the fabric position, open out the remaining fold. The backing should be wrong side up and should be hanging evenly on all sides of the table.

3. Lay the folded batting on top so it covers one-quarter of the backing surface. Use a ruler to double-check that the quarter folded center corner matches the center of the backing (see the photo below on the right). Unfold the batting to cover one-half of the surface (see the top left photo on page 183), and then unfold again to cover the full surface. (If you must work alone, telephone books or other weights will help hold things in place as you unfold.)

4. Lay the folded quilt top on top of the batting (see the top right photo on page 183), matching centers, and unfold it in the same way until the quilt is completely layered. The right side of the quilt top should be facing up. Double-check all the way around the table to make sure that the three layers are even and centered.

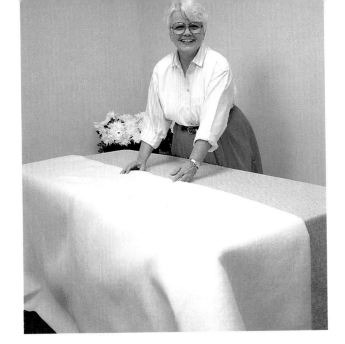

Pinning

A minimum of 350 safety pins (I like the rustproof chrome-plated #1s) is needed to pin-baste a queen/double bed quilt; a crib quilt takes at least 75. The actual number of pins depends on how complicated the quilting is, whether the batting is polyester or cotton (cotton is less slippery, so you can get by with fewer pins), and your experience. Start with more than you think you need, and reduce the number when it feels comfortable.

Begin pinning from the center out (see the photo below). When the first line of pins is secure, stop, put one hand on the center of the table, and reach under the quilt to the backing and gently tug to make sure no wrinkles developed as you added the batting and quilt top. As you pin, keep the quilting pattern in mind so you don't pin too close to the intended stitching lines. It's worse than a nuisance if the presser foot catches on a pin and distorts your stitch.

One of the real advantages of pinning over hand-basting is that you do not have to constantly put your hand under the quilt. Just pin from the top, and when you feel the pin point touch the tabletop, pull it back up through the quilt. I used to close each pin individually, but now I insert a dozen or so and then go back and close them with the Kwik Klose handle (see the photo below). Then I sprinkle a few more pins around and keep going.

TIP: Leave Safety Pins Open

When you remove the safety pins from your quilt, leave them open. You will save one closing and one opening each use. It doesn't seem like much until you multiply two times 300 pins and think of the abuse that can be to your fingers.

When the entire table surface is pinned, gently pull the quilt to one side and pin a new section (see the top left photo on page 185). Every time that you change the position, check the back to make sure no wrinkles are developing. When you are done, turn the whole thing over and check the back to make sure it is as smooth as possible.

If you did not do so previously, now is a good time to trim the excess batting and backing to 2 inches beyond the quilt edge (see the top right photo on page 185). Trimming reduces both the weight and the size of the quilt. It is amazing how much extra batting and backing weigh, especially cotton batting. Any reduction in size makes the quilt easier to handle. I don't trim closer than 2 inches because I usually want at least ⅜ inch beyond the quilt to roll into the binding. Also, if you do very much quilting in the border, you need this much edge to hold.

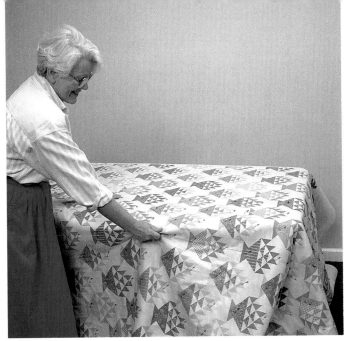

Packaging

This is the point at which most people think, "I still don't understand how you get this great big quilt through that little opening." The trick is to teach the quilt who is in control. Generally, I want to stitch the long vertical center seam first. So I roll up the part of the quilt that will be to the right of that seam at the machine, stopping just a few inches from the seam (see the photo below).

To the left of the seam, I fold the quilt in 8- to 9-inch folds until just a few inches from the center seam (see the left photo below). Now you have a long, skinny quilt. Keeping the roll on your right and the folded section on your left, start rolling the quilt from one end securely. When you are done, the whole thing is not much bigger than a packaged quilt batt and you are the one in control (see the right photo below). Use the same method to package a quilt for diagonal seams. The difference is that you will have a very long quilt before the last roll is complete.

AT THE MACHINE

At last you are ready to sit down at the machine and sew a full-sized quilt. You have already set up your machine, extra tables, and general work area following the advice in Chapters 3 and 7. Your machine is properly threaded, and you've checked the tension by sewing a sample. Everything is set so that you can take your rolled quilt directly to the machine and begin.

Position the quilt with the first center seam under the presser foot. Hold the quilt roll in your lap and unroll enough of the quilt so that there is no tension on the section where you will be sewing. Begin sewing, redistributing the quilt as you go so that the feed dogs are not forced to pull the entire weight (see the left photo below). The quilt can hang on chairs, on tables beside or in front of you, or over your shoulder (see the right photo below). Or you can try the new V-drape position.

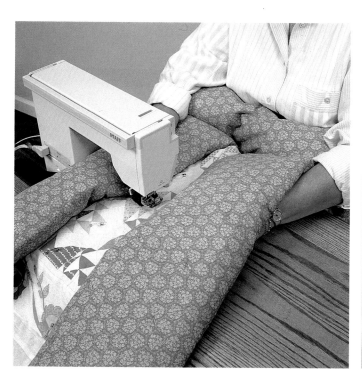
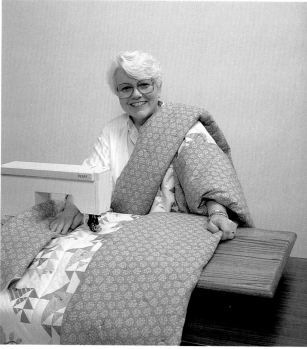

Reroll and Relax

Whenever you stop to reroll the quilt, do some stretching exercises to relax your back, neck, and shoulders. Take some deep breaths. Focus your eyes on another color and object. The quilt is heavier and bulkier than most things you work on at the machine, and the rows of stitching are longer and require more concentration. You'll do better if you stop and stretch your muscles periodically.

If you are feeling too tired to refold or repackage the quilt properly, stop and rest for a longer period. You are much more likely to make a mistake when you are tired. Chances are you may unintentionally stitch a section of the backing into a seam where it does not belong!

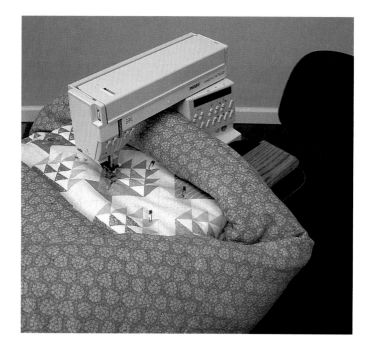

The V-Drape Position The V-drape position requires table space to the left of the machine. It works very nicely if your machine is in a cabinet with a lid that opens out. Instead of holding the quilt in your lap, unroll more of the quilt and at lap level make a V-fold so that the quilt is on the table to the left of the needle (see the photo above). Keep adjusting the fold as you progress down the seam. Just don't let it drape too much, or the feed dogs will have to pull the weight of the quilt up and over the edge.

Stitching Order While I generally stitch a few vertical rows and then a few horizontal rows, it is more habit than necessity. My experience has been that there is no magic stitching order. However, some people swear that you must start at the center of each row and work out or alternate the direction of every other row or follow some other complex arrangement. Do whatever works best for you.

After the main horizontal and vertical lines are quilted, you can move on to any planned quilting on the borders. On some quilts you can bind the edges at this point, which eliminates excess weight, decreases the size, and covers the batting so it can't snag on jewelry or rough skin. (If there is a chance your quilting is not going to be balanced—perhaps you plan a very dense filler in one area and less dense quilting in another area—hold off on binding until you proceed further.)

Scrolling As long as you are quilting in the same direction, you can repackage the quilt without completely removing it from the machine. After completing one row, clip the threads and move the quilt so that the center of the seam just stitched is close to the needle. Now, thinking of the quilt as a scroll, unroll the right side to expose the next seam you want to quilt. Fold the left side and roll up the end as before. Reposition the quilt at the start of the seam.

The neater the package for the first quilted seam, the more times you can scroll or repackage at the machine. I usually can do one, sometimes two seams on either side of the center before I have to reroll the quilt completely. Every time I have to repackage completely, I change the direction that I am quilting and I turn the quilt over to make sure there are no puckers or problems in the backing.

Stitching in the Ditch The same in-the-ditch guidelines (page 19) used for smaller pieces work on larger packaged quilts too. Be careful not to distort the seam line when pulling seams apart for stitching. The seam should extend straight in front of the needle. If it is wavy or curving, you will not achieve straight quilting lines. It sounds obvious when you read about it, but it is not so obvious when sewing. Machine quilting is not forgiving.

When I am quilting in the ditch with invisible thread, I like to take my basting pins out as I go. It helps me keep track of which seams I have quilted, reduces the potential for snags, and is one less pin I may forget to remove later.

Free-Motion Quilting Specific information about how to do free-motion quilting is in Chapter 7. Most quilts have a few long, straight lines that need to be quilted, even if there is considerable free-motion quilting. I prefer to do those long, straight lines with machine-guided in-the-ditch stitching. Packaging for free-motion quilting is generally the same, except when you need to make a larger area available for quilting.

What About the Thread Ends? Occasionally, I see quilts on display with long threads dangling all over the quilt. I know the quilt maker means it as an artistic statement, but I find it a fulfillment of my fantasy not to have to deal with thread ends.

It doesn't matter whether you take a tiny backstitch or stitch in place as you start a row of machine-guided quilting, but you should do something to anchor your stitching. Trim off loose thread ends frequently to prevent them from getting caught in subsequent rows of quilting. In the interior of the quilt, I pull the threads to the back before clipping, even though I have stitched in place.

With free-motion quilting, you can hold the fabric still for a few stitches to secure them. If the thread doesn't seem secure, pull both threads to the back, knot them, and then draw them back into the quilt with a hand-quilting needle so that they can lodge in the batting.

11

BORDERS, BINDINGS, AND QUILT FINISHING

You might already have enough blocks for a quilt top, or you may plan to practice machine quilting on a small piece of user-friendly printed patchwork fabric. No matter what the project, if you are at the point of adding borders to a quilt you plan to machine-quilt, this chapter provides several options. Choose the method you prefer, although I hope you will want to try them all at some time. The border instructions are followed by methods for binding and finishing your quilt.

PREPARING THE QUILT

Diagram 1

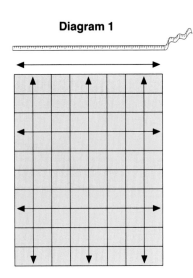

Before adding borders it is important to measure your quilt carefully and accurately. Measure the length from point to point (Diagram 1). If you squared up each of the blocks properly before the final assembly, the quilt sides should match and the corners should be square. If the sides don't match, make the needed adjustments now. If you let it go, the error will just become more exaggerated with each border you add.

If the difference in length between the two quilt sides is slight, ease the longer side by machine-basting until it matches the shorter side. If the quilt seems to be wrinkling, it means there is too much fabric to ease. You will have to correct the problem by altering some of the quilt seams instead. It is most important that opposite sides be precisely the same length.

BORDER DECISIONS

Before You Cut

The border widths for each quilt shown in this book are given in the project directions. Your first step is to decide if the number and width of the borders are appropriate for the quilt you made. Feel free to design your own borders using fabrics you choose. Borders should be designed to extend your quilt to the desired finished size and to make the quilt as attractive as possible.

Before you cut, lay the quilt top interior on a flat surface and arrange pieces of the planned border fabrics around one corner. Step back, squint, and make sure you like the arrangement. (Squinting gives you the illusion of seeing the quilt from a greater distance—as if from across the room or down the hall: Does it still look great or does it die?) Sometimes just changing the width of the fabrics or rearranging their order is all that's needed to arrive at a pleasing configuration, but other times, it's back to the store!

To Miter or Not to Miter

Very few of my quilts have mitered corners. Even when you think you see them in my books, they are usually mock-mitered. (When a true mitered binding pops up, you know someone else finished the quilt.)

Mitered corners take more time, more fabric, more skill, and lots more luck than blunt corners. If you are making quilts to enter into competition, it is a good idea to become expert at mitering. Mitering doesn't make the quilt warmer or more loved, but it is more likely to satisfy the judges. My quilts are made for everyday use, not competition. When the same nondirectional fabric is used for the entire border, the resulting corners look the same whether they are blunt-seamed or mitered (Diagram 2).

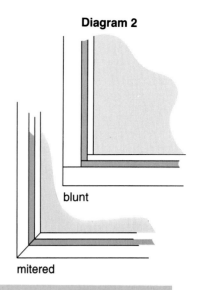

Diagram 2

blunt

mitered

My Mitering Quota Theory

I believe we are all born with an unknown quota for the number of perfect mitered corners we can make in a lifetime. I would hate to be 85 years old and have a great striped fabric that just had to be mitered and discover that I had used up my quota mitering something as undemanding as muslin. So I save my mitering for corners where it really counts. A corollary to this theory is, "Only three out of four mitered corners can be perfect on the same quilt on the first try!"

MAKING MITERED AND MOCK MITERED CORNERS

Borders that will be mitered have to be cut longer than blunt finish borders. When cutting blunt borders, the length of the top and bottom border is calculated by adding the width of the quilt plus the width of two finished borders plus ½ inch. That is the way to calculate the length of all (top, bottom, and side) borders with mitered corners. They must be positioned perfectly and sewn to the side of the quilt, stopping ¼ inch from the end of the quilt. Press the seam allowance toward quilt top.

To stitch a traditional miter, the quilt is folded at a 45-degree angle with the borders perfectly aligned on top of each other. Continue the fold line with the stitching (Diagram 3). This is only compatible with traditional layering.

For a mock miter, work from the top of the quilt with one border extended flat and the other folded and pressed to make a perfect 45-degree angle. Pin the folded strip in place and carefully stitch by hand with a hidden stitch (Diagram 4).

When all four corners are completed to satisfaction, trim away the excess fabric and proceed. It is okay to miter one border, perhaps a demanding stripe, and not the others.

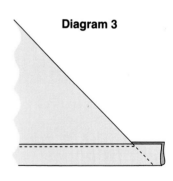

Diagram 3

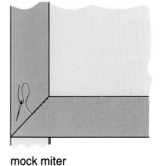

Diagram 4

mock miter

FLAPS

A flap is a finishing detail I love. Just like a very narrow border, a flap adds a tiny bit of color that accents or delineates the adjacent

Diagram 5

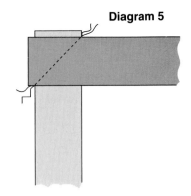

TIP: Piecing Borders or Binding Strips

Regardless of the method chosen, cut the border strips on the lengthwise grain if possible. If you must piece the borders or binding, place
the pieces at right angles and stitch diagonally as if you were piecing
bias strips (Diagram 5). The seams will appear less visible, and bindings
will have less bulk when folded.

fabrics. Just as an extra mat with a colored edge can dress up a
framed picture, a flap can perk up a quilt. Flaps can appear between borders or next to the binding. In sewing terminology, a
flap might be described as piping without the cord.

While the flap looks like it is tucked between two layers of fabric when a seam is sewn, it isn't. It must be added separately, just
as if it were a border; otherwise the corners won't overlap
correctly.

Making a Flap To make a flap, cut the flap strip twice as wide as
the desired finished width, plus ½ inch for seam allowances. The
most common width of flap that I use is ¼ inch, which means I
cut the strips 1 inch wide. Cut on the straight grain unless you
want the decorative effect of bias. Fold and press in half lengthwise with wrong sides facing. Align raw edges of the flap with
the raw edges of the last section of the quilt and sew it in position. The flap may encroach on the piece it is lying on, but I have
never found that objectionable. After adding flap strips in the
same order as border strips, proceed with the next border or
binding.

When you insert a ¼-inch finished border, stitching down both
sides, any deviation in the straightness of the seams is very visible. This does not happen with flaps. Also, the little bit of dimension that a flap provides is always very interesting.

FOUR WAYS TO ADD BORDERS

Each quilt in this book is finished with one of the four border
methods. Most quilt books stick to the Good Old-fashioned Way.
The more quilts you make, the more opportunities you will have
to incorporate the other three techniques. The method I use most
I call Modified Quilt-As-You-Sew.

The Good Old-fashioned Way

In traditional quilt making, borders are added to the quilt top before any layering or quilting is done. In fact, most quilters probably consider a quilt top unfinished if the borders are not in place.
Some people cut a long strip of border fabric, sew it from one end
of the quilt to the other, and cut off the excess. This is a "no-no"!
Always cut the borders the exact desired finished length plus
seam allowances and make the quilt fit the borders. If you have
decided to miter the corners, each border must be cut the full
length of its respective side plus the width of two adjoining borders. It is safer to allow a little extra fabric, but still mark the exact

length on the border and make it fit the quilt. If you have followed instructions, you will have already measured the quilt interior in several places to make sure the quilt is a consistent width and length and the corners are square. Here's how to proceed from there to make perfect blunt-border corners:

1. Cut the first pair of lengthwise borders (for the sides of the quilt) the exact length of the quilt interior. Even though I do very little pinning in my quilt making, this is one place where I usually mark and match halves and quarters on the quilt and border before I stitch. When stitched, press seams toward the borders.

2. Now measure the crosswise ends, including the newly attached borders. Cut the first pair of crosswise borders the exact length. Pin and stitch in place. Press seams toward the borders. The quilt with its first set of borders should have square corners and matching side-to-side dimensions, not just at the corners, but throughout the quilt.

3. Continue adding the borders in the same way. For more attractive corners, continue adding the lengthwise borders first and then the crosswise. This order also means the length of the borders will be closer to equal, which usually makes cutting more economical.

Standard Quilt-As-You-Sew Borders

Quilt-As-You-Sew blocks like those in the Virginia Reel (page 52) automatically require Quilt-As-You-Sew borders. If you have just finished the interior of a Quilt-As-You-Sew quilt, you are familiar with the finishing strips used to cover raw seams. This method for adding borders encases the raw edges so no finishing strips are required. Subsequent borders are added stitch and flip. Surface quilting, if any, is done after the borders are added.

Preparing the Border Backing and Border Batting The border batting and border backing strips cover the **total** width of all the front borders; therefore, they are cut wide enough to accommodate all the multiple borders. The first border is added to the quilt at the same time as the border batting and backing. Any subsequent borders are added with the stitch and flip method.

When finishing the quilt with a separate binding, the border batting and border backing pieces are cut to extend about 1½ inches beyond the **last** border; batting and backing will be trimmed when adding the binding. For quilts with a single border, the batting and border backing are cut 1½ inches wider than the border, assuming a separate binding.

Cut the border backing and border batting pieces needed for your quilt. The width is determined by the total finished width of all borders, plus 1¾ inches. The lengths are the same as the first border in step 1 below.

Adding the First Border To add the first border

1. Measure your quilt. Cut two side borders the desired border width plus ½ inch for seam allowances and the exact length of the quilt. Cut two end borders. The length of the top and bot-

tom borders is the width of the quilt top, plus twice the desired finished border (both sides) width plus ½ inch for seam allowances.

When adding multiple borders to a quilt, always complete one round of borders before measuring and cutting the next fabric.

2. Add the side borders first. Lay the quilt on a large, flat surface right side up, and put one of the side border pieces on top, right side down with one long edge lined up with the long edge of the quilt. Mark and match the center point and quarter points of both the quilt and the border. Pin in place sparingly.

3. To add the entire batting and border backing fabric, fold the edge of the quilt you are working on forward about 15 inches. Lay the backing fabric strip against the backing of the quilt, right sides facing. Put the batting on top of it. Line up raw edges and ends, then pin securely in place through all six layers (Diagram 6).

4. Repeat steps 2 and 3 on the opposite long edge of the quilt.

5. Machine-stitch ¼ inch from the raw edges of both sides, through all six layers, the entire length of the quilt. Remove all pins.

6. Trim away any excess batting from the seams to reduce bulk, but do not trim closer than ⅛ inch; otherwise the batting will tend to pull out of the seam. Layer the front border, batting, and border backing together, pulling them away from the quilt interior, so they lie flat and line up with the quilt top. The batting is now sandwiched between the border and the border backing fabric. This is one seam I recommend pressing, preferably with steam.

7. Position the end pieces (top and bottom) of the first border, border backing, and batting as shown (Diagram 7). The two

Diagram 6

Diagram 7

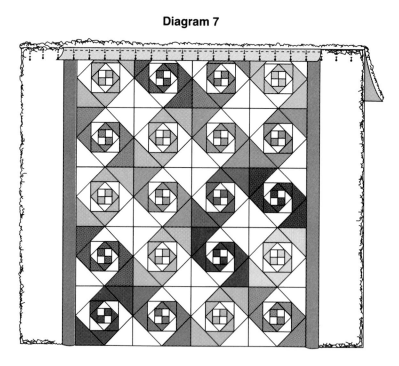

strips of border fabric end even with the outer edges of the side border strips while the batting and border backing extend the full width of the finished quilt. Trim the border ends to the exact length of the side border as necessary. Pin securely, machine-stitch, trim the excess batting from the seam allowance, and pull the borders forward, as in steps 2 through 6. Press the seam. Repeat on the other end.

Adding Subsequent Borders Now that the first border, the batting, and the border backings are in place, adding subsequent borders is quick and easy with the stitch-and-flip method. Always attach the side borders first and complete one set of borders before starting the next.

1. Pin the first borders flat. Along one long edge, place a strip of the second border fabric on top of first border, right sides facing, raw edges matching, and pin them securely. The second side border should line up where the first border stops (Diagram 8).

Diagram 8

2. Machine-stitch through both borders, the batting, and the backing fabric ¼ inch from the raw edges where the two borders meet. Align and stitch the opposite side border to the quilt in the same manner. After removing the pins, open the second border outward to lie flat on the batting. Press.

3. Add the second border to both top and bottom ends of the quilt. These strips go from one end of the second side border to the other.

4. Repeat for remaining borders.

Adding a Quilt-As-You-Sew Border with Corner Blocks Add side border strips as above. Cut the top and bottom borders ½ inch longer than the width of the quilt before borders, then cut four contrasting squares the cut width of the border. Sew one square to each end of the top and bottom border strips. Matching seams carefully, sew top and bottom borders to quilt (Diagram 9).

Modified Quilt-As-You-Sew Borders

This method is suitable for nearly any traditionally pieced and layered quilt. Instead of adding borders to the quilt top and then layering and quilting, the smaller patchwork interior (without borders) is centered on the full-sized backing and batting. After the interior is quilted, Quilt-As-You-Sew borders are added all around. The method is the same stitch-and-flip approach used to add subsequent borders in the Standard Quilt-As-You-Sew border. It eliminates several rows of stitching and reduces bulk when machine-quilting the interior section; and this one seam is doing the work of two, quilting while you piece.

1. Calculate the size of the quilt top plus the finished sizes of all the borders. Cut the batting and backing 2 inches bigger all around. Center the quilt top on top of the batting and backing and quilt the interior.

2. Measure and cut the quilt borders. Cut the first pair of lengthwise borders (for the sides of the quilt) the exact length of the quilt interior and desired finished width plus ½ inch for seam allowances. The length of the top and bottom borders is the width of the quilt top, plus twice the desired finished border width plus ½ inch for seam allowances. Again, unless I have a fabric or design that demands mitering, I find crossed or blunt borders to be just fine.

3. After the quilt interior is quilted, put it right side up on a large flat surface. Add the side borders first and then the ends, just as if you were adding borders before layering and quilting. When there are several borders, I prefer to add them one at a time to create more quilting. Put the first side border right side down on top of the quilt just as if you were making a regular seam (Diagram 10). Pin in place. Stitch through all thicknesses, quilting and seaming at the same time. Repeat with the opposite side border. Open new borders flat into the proper position before adding borders on the ends of the quilt. Pin or very lightly press the first border flat before seaming across the end of it with another border.

Attaching Previously Quilted Borders

Previously quilted borders can be added with finishing strips, or the inner edge of the border can be left unquilted until after joining. See the Stippled Postage Stamp Quilt on page 110.

196

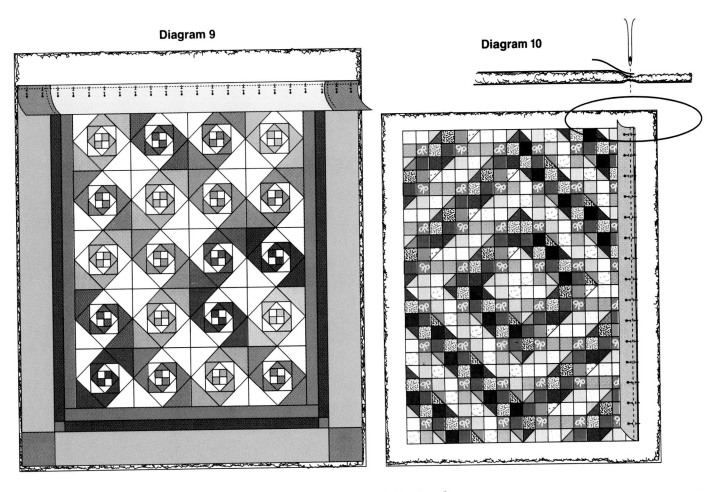

Diagram 9

Diagram 10

Cutting and Marking the Borders To cut and mark the borders

1. Cut strips of border fabric the desired width plus seam allowances. Cut backing and batting strips 1½ inches wider than the cut width of the border strips. Measure your quilt to determine the length to cut the borders, backing, and batting strips. Cut the first pair of lengthwise strips (for the sides of the quilt) the exact length of the quilt interior. The length of the top and bottom strips is the width of the quilt top, plus twice the desired finished border width plus ½ inch for seam allowances.

2. Transfer the quilting pattern to the right side of the border fabric.

3. In order to make any necessary adjustments easier, work on the top and bottom borders after the side borders are marked, quilted, and attached to the quilt. You may even choose to mark both corners, but leave one unquilted until the border is attached, so any final adjustments can be made more easily.

Quilting and Adding the Borders To quilt and add the borders

1. Always quilt the borders before sewing them to the quilt. Layer the border fabric, right side up on top of the batting and backing, wrong side up. Align raw edges where the border will be joined to the quilt. (The batting and backing will extend approximately 1½ inches beyond the border fabric along the outside edge.) Baste or pin the layers together.

2. Quilt as desired. I suggest you begin by quilting any straight lines first.

3. Place the border and quilt top right sides facing, with the border on top. Pull back the top layer of fabric, which is the border backing. Stitch through the remaining five layers of fabric and batting. The quilted border is joined to the quilt top with the same method as that used for Quilt-As-You-Sew Block Assembly Without Finishing Strips (page 116).

4. Working from the underside, secure the loose edge of border backing fabric. Turn under the edges of the backing even with the stitching line where the border was added. Slip-stitch in place. Complete quilting at the inner edge of the border.

THE FRENCH-FOLD BLUNT-CORNER BINDING

Throughout this book I have stressed making decisions after considering different options. When it comes to binding the edge of a quilt, however, the blunt-corner French-fold binding is the only method I intend to discuss. If I were entering my quilts in competition, I would take the time to make a continuous binding with mitered corners. Not because I like it better, it makes the quilt warmer, or it means I love the recipient of the quilt more, but because I know most score sheets give more points for mitered-corner continuous bindings.

A French-fold binding is a double-fold and is generally cut on the straight grain. It is cut four times as wide as the desired finished width plus ½ inch for two seam allowances and ⅛ inch to ¼ inch more to go around the thickness of the quilt. The fatter the batt, the more you need to allow here. My favorite finished width is whatever size I think looks best on the quilt. Some quilts need a subtle, narrow binding, and others look best with a large, high-contrast binding. The most common width, about ½ inch, requires the equivalent of ⅝ yard of fabric for a standard-size quilt.

Just as with borders, I prefer to cut the binding on the lengthwise grain (unless I need bias for a curved edge). Measure the quilt side and add 2 to 3 inches to determine the length for binding. The excess will be trimmed later, but it makes adding the binding more relaxed. I avoid piecing bindings whenever possible, but if you must piece, be sure to do it diagonally, as for borders (page 192).

Stabilizing the Quilt

Unless the quilting runs very close to the edge, it is a good idea to stabilize the quilt before adding the binding. Machine-baste a scant ¼ inch from the raw edge of the quilt top through all the layers around all four sides. The excess batting and backing are cut away later.

Interestingly, even though I machine-piece and -quilt almost every quilt I make, I still love a hand-finished binding. That is, the binding is sewn onto the right side of the quilt by machine and wrapped around the edge to the back, where I stitch it down by hand.

Attaching the Binding

To attach the binding

1. Fold the binding strip in half lengthwise with the wrong sides facing and the raw edges even. Press. Binding strips are added in the same order as borders, sides first, then top and bottom strips.

2. Lay the binding on the quilt so that both raw edges of binding match the raw edge of the quilt top, and machine-stitch in place.

3. To determine how much excess backing and batting to trim away, pull one section of binding flat, so it extends onto the excess batting. Because I like full-feeling bindings, I trim the backing and batting to be almost as wide as the extended binding. In other words, the extended binding will be about $\frac{3}{16}$ inch wider than the backing and batting when trimmed (Diagram 11). Assume you start with a $2\frac{5}{8}$-inch-wide binding strip and measure from the seam, not the edge of the binding, then you trim the batting and backing $\frac{7}{8}$ inch from the seam line or $\frac{5}{8}$ inch from the edge of the quilt.

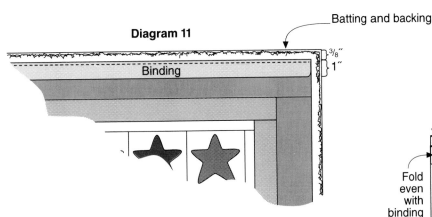

Diagram 11

Batting and backing

Binding

$\frac{3}{8}$"

1"

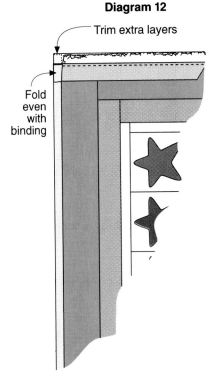

Diagram 12

Trim extra layers

Fold even with binding

4. Roll the extra batting and binding around the raw edge of the quilt to the back, and hand-stitch in place, using the row of machine stitching as a stabilizer and a guide

   The hand hemming stitch I use is hidden. The needle comes out of the quilt, takes a bite of the binding, and re-enters the quilt exactly behind the stitch. The thread is carried in the layers of quilt, not on the outside.

5. Make blunt corners (I feel mitered corners aren't necessary on most bindings) by completing the hand stitching on the sides of the quilt before beginning the ends. Trim batting out of the last $\frac{1}{2}$ inch of side binding (Diagram 12) before completing the hand stitching. In a staggered fashion trim away other excess pieces of fabric so that the corners are not bulky or thicker than the rest of the binding.

6. Measure the quilt ends carefully. Cut binding strips, adding $\frac{1}{2}$ inch at each end. To eliminate raw edges, fold under the extra $\frac{1}{2}$ inch at each end before folding the strips in half lengthwise. Continue in the same manner as earlier.

7. Complete the hand stitching for the top and bottom ends of the quilt. At the corners, trim away enough batting and seam allowances to make the corners feel and look like the same thickness as the rest of the binding. Carefully stitch ends shut.

TIP: Machine-Hemming a Binding

To hem a binding by machine, stitch it to the quilt back using the stabilizing stitching as a guideline. Bring the binding to the front and either topstitch with invisible thread or experiment with your machine's hemming stitch. The hemming stitch will make several straight stitches in the quilt, followed by a V-shaped stitch that veers off to nip and secure the binding (Diagram 13). On many machines, the buttonhole stitch can be adjusted to create a tiny stitch for hemming (on the Pfaff 1400 series, it is program #14). I push the double-needle position to overcome the computer-set width and create a very tiny stitch. On programmable machines, I have created my own stitch, which I like better. It goes four stitches forward and then takes a tiny bite (Diagram 13).

Diagram 13

Hemming   Buttonhole
stitch   stitch

FINISHING TOUCHES

The Hanging Sleeve

The most popular method of displaying a quilt is to stitch a sleeve, or casing, onto the backing of the quilt. When a rod or dowel is slipped through the sleeve, the quilt's weight is evenly distributed and no section receives undue stress.

To make a sleeve, cut a strip of fabric 2 inches longer than the quilt edge by 9 inches wide. Turn both short ends under 1½ inches and topstitch. Fold the strip in half lengthwise, wrong sides facing, and sew the long raw edges in a ¼-inch seam. Press the seam allowance open so it runs down the middle of the sleeve (Diagram 14). Center the sleeve along the top edge of the quilt backing, approximately 1 inch below the binding, with the seam face down (Diagram 15). Sew the sleeve to the quilt through the backing and batting along both long edges.

Diagram 14   **Diagram 15**

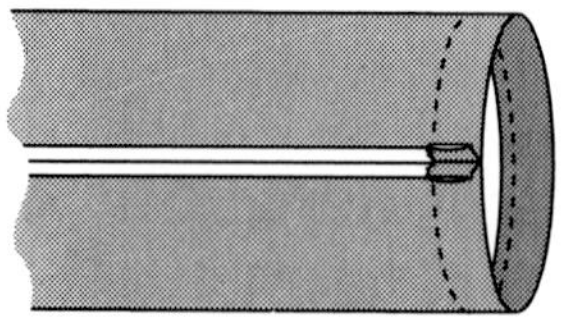

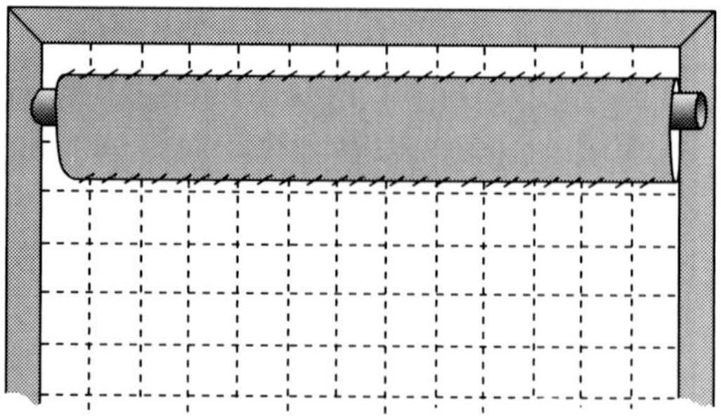

Signing Your Quilt

It's not done until it is signed. More and more machines feature fancy stitches, alphabets, and monogram capabilities. Play with the possibilities to add creative interest to the labels for your quilts.

RESOURCES

Ask for the products discussed in this book at local fabric, craft, or quilting stores. If you are unsuccessful in finding the products, feel free to pass the manufacturer's address on to your local store. Addresses and phone numbers change, but at press time, these were accurate. If there have been any changes since that time, we regret any inconvenience. At the end of the list of manufacturers, I have given a few of the companies that are in the mail order business.

PRODUCTS MENTIONED IN THIS BOOK

Barbara Johannah's books, including *Continuous Curve Quilting*, from Purchase for Less; 231 Floresta BJB; Portola Valley, CA 94028

Hari Walner's *Continuous Line Quilting Patterns*, from Beautiful Publications; 13340 Harrison Street; Thornton, CO 80241-1403

Harriet Hargrave's books and many machine-quilting supplies, from Harriet's Treadle Arts, a retail store at 6390 W. 44th; Wheat Ridge, CO 88003 (also sells by mail)

Kaleidoscope Toy, from Homecrafters Manufacturing Corporation; 1859 Kenion Point; Snellville, GA 30278

Light Tables, from Me Sew, Inc.; 24307 Magic Mountain Pkwy, Suite 195; Valencia, CA 91355

Sewing machine table, from Douglas Products; P.O. Box 2606; Rohnert Park, CA 94927

MANUFACTURERS MENTIONED

Batting Companies

Fairfield Processing Corp.; P.O. Box 1157; Danbury, CT 06813

Hobbs Bonded Fibers; P.O. Box 2521; Waco, TX 76702

Warm Products, Inc.; 16120 Woodinville-Redmond Road, #4; Woodinville, WA 98072

Other Manufacturers

Fabric Traditions; 1350 Broadway, Suite 2106; New York, NY 10018

Gammill Quilting Machine Co.; 1452 West Gibson Street; West Plains, MO 65775 (for commercial quilting machines)

Sulky of America; 3113 Broadpoint Drive; Harbor Heights, FL 33983 (for Sulky Threads)

MAIL ORDER RESOURCES

Mostly Quilting Supplies, Including Fabrics, Books, Batting, and Notions

Keepsake Quilting; Route 25B; P.O. Box 1618; Centre Harbor, NH 03226-1618 (or call 603-253-8731)

Quilts & Other Comforts; 6700 West 44th Avenue; P.O. Box 394; Wheat Ridge, CO 80034-0394 (or call 303-420-4272)

Mostly Quilting but No Fabric

Treadleart; 25834 Narbonne; Lomita, CA 90717 (or call 310-534-5122)

Full-Line Sewing Catalogues, with Some Emphasis on Quilting

Clotilde; 2 Sew Smart Way, B8301; Stevens Point, WI 54481-8031 (or call 800-772-2891 M–F 7:30 A.M. to 4:00 P.M. Central time)

Nancy's Notions; P.O. Box 683; Beaver Dam, WI 53916-0683 (or call 800-833-0690 M–F 7 A.M. to 9 P.M. and Sat. 8 A.M. to 4 P.M. Central time)

INDEX